Clueless in the Kitchen

A Cookbook for Teens

EVELYN RAAB

There's everything to eat here

FIREFLY BOOKS

For my sons, Dustin and Jared, who are definitely not clueless in the kitchen, and for my husband, George, who unfortunately is.

Thank you also to my intrepid platoon of recipe testers: Sarah Chalmers, Sarah Nashman, and Benjamin Rowland, without whom I would never have believed that it was really possible to make such weird cooking mistakes. And to my mother, in whose kitchen I was allowed to make mine.

A FIREFLY BOOK

Published by Firefly Books Ltd. 1998

Sixth printing 2008

Publisher Cataloging–in–Publication Data (U.S.)
(Library of Congress Standards)

Raab, Evelyn
       Clueless in the kitchen : a cookbook for teens

ISBN-13: 978-1-55209-224-8
ISBN-10: 1-55209-224-0

1. Cookery.   I. Title.

TX652.R32   1998   641.5′12   C97-932380-0

First published in Canada by Key Porter Books Limited

Published in the United States by
Firefly Books (U.S.) Inc.
P.O. Box 1338
Ellicott Station
Buffalo, New York, USA
14205

Illustrations: George Walker
Design: Jean Lightoot Peters
Electronic formatting: Heidi Palfrey

Printed and bound in Canada

Clueless in the Kitchen

Contents

Starting from Scratch

How you ended up with this book is not important. Maybe your parents gave it to you. Maybe you bought it for yourself. Maybe you found it in a ditch. It doesn't matter. The thing is, you have it, and now you have to use it. But how?

Well, OK, this is a cookbook. You've probably already noticed that. And it's full of recipes—which is pretty much what you'd expect. These recipes are simple without being stupid. They contain no scary terminology, no really strange ingredients, no complicated procedures. They also contain (almost) no processed foods—no cake mixes, no condensed tomato soup, no frozen whipped topping. You don't need them. Ever. Cooking from scratch is easy, cheap, and *always* tastes better. Really.

This book is also full of basic kitchen stuff that no one has ever bothered to tell you. Or maybe you weren't listening. And now you're sorry, because *now* you want to know. *Now* the kitchen drain is plugged, or you want to cut up a chicken, or you have to—yikes— defrost the freezer. And you *certainly* don't want to go crawling back to

Mom, do you? There's also information on how to shop, where to get kitchen equipment, and how to plan a meal.

So how do you get started? Well, just start. Find something you want to cook and cook it. Go ahead—be daring. Cooking isn't, after all, brain surgery. It just *looks* that way.

Key to Icons

The following icons are used to identify the different sorts of recipes. A recipe may have several icons or symbols, suggesting that it falls into many categories—such as cheap and vegetarian, or Mom food and family dinner, or whatever.

Cheap Eats

Oh, stop feeling so sorry for yourself. Everyone is broke sometimes. Eating cheaply doesn't mean eating bad food. It doesn't have to mean surviving on a dreary menu of canned beans and bologna, boxed macaroni-and-cheese dinners, and day-old doughnuts. Unless, of course, you want it to. But that's your business.

Learn to cook and you'll *always* eat well without spending a fortune. Some of the best things in life, after all, are cheap.

Mom Food

Who fed you chicken soup when you had a cold? Who waited for you after school with homemade cookies? Who made the best potato salad on the block? Well, OK, so maybe your mom wasn't really much of a cook. And maybe she was too busy driving a backhoe to be around after school. And maybe you never had a bowl of homemade chicken soup in your life. It's *never* too late for Mom Food. Even if you have to make it yourself.

Vegetarian Stuff

Being a vegetarian doesn't just mean picking all the pepperoni off your take-out pizza, or ordering your fries *without* gravy. No, really, you *are* going to have to learn to cook a few things, if you want your parents to stop freaking out.

Cooking to Impress

Most of the time, cooking is a pretty practical business. You cook because you're hungry and you want something to eat. You might make a pot of chili, or a casserole, or some other normal regular food. But then there are other times. Birthdays. Anniversaries. Groundhog Day. Or maybe you have an ulterior motive. Maybe you figure a romantic evening over a fondue pot will do the trick. Well, maybe it will.

Couch Potato Food

You wander around the house with that "I need something to eat but I don't know what" look on your face. You open the fridge, the pantry, a drawer. No, you don't want leftover tuna casserole, or a bowl of soup, or a slice of toast with peanut butter. You need something interesting. Something delicious. Something you can eat in front of the TV. With your hands. No plate.

You need Couch Potato Food.

For heaven's sake, use a napkin at least.

Dinner for the Family

Drat. It's 5 p.m. and there's no one home. There's no stew bubbling on the stove, no casserole baking in the oven, no apple pie cooling on the counter. There is, however, a package of hamburger in the fridge, a bag of macaroni in the pantry, and a note on the table that says, "I'll be home at 7. Make dinner. Love, Mom." So what's a kid supposed to do?

Well, cook, I guess.

How to Cook Absolutely Anything

Read the recipe. Twice. The first time you read it to find out if this actually sounds like something you want to cook. Or eat. Does it include an ingredient you hate? Does it require a piece of equipment you don't have? Does it take too long to cook? The second time, read the recipe c-a-r-e-f-u-l-l-y. Go through all the ingredients. Do you have them? Are you *sure*? Didn't your brother eat all the chocolate chips last week? Go check. Now.

Assemble everything you need before you start. Everything. The bowls, the pots, the measuring cups, all the ingredients. Take *nothing* for granted. You don't want to discover, at a critical moment, that the 9-inch baking dish you need is in the freezer, half filled with last week's leftover lasagna.

Follow the recipe exactly. This is no place to be rebellious. At least, not the first time. Do it once *exactly* the way the recipe tells you to. Just once. The next time, go ahead and be reckless. Leave out the tomatoes! Double the walnuts! Heck—add some peanut butter! It's your recipe now, baby.

Get over it. Everyone has disasters. Don't wallow in them. Pick yourself up, scrape the burnt crud off the bottom of the oven, mop up the mess on the floor, feed the disintegrated glop to the dog. And get on with life. It happens.

Know what you like. You can't cook if you don't know what you like to eat. And eating, after all, is the end result. Or, at least, it's supposed to be. Know what you enjoy eating, cook what you want to eat, and you'll probably have fun doing it.

And finally, there are no rules. No one owns a recipe, and there is no right and wrong way for something to taste. If you like it, then it's good. If you don't like it, then it's not good. That's all there is to it. Trust yourself.

The Kitchen—A Guide to Alien Territory

Welcome to the kitchen. Are you nervous? You should be. Your kitchen is a place so dangerous, so intimidating, so full of potential disaster that it's really no place for beginners. But here you are anyway. So, let's try to be brave, shall we?

Everywhere you look, in an average kitchen, there are things that can go terribly wrong. And they will. Appliances will self-destruct, bacteria will multiply, gross stuff will happen. So you might as well know how to deal with it. And no whining.

Is this your very first solo kitchen? Then it's even more overwhelming. First you have to get everything you need, then you have to cope with it all. And then (yikes) you're expected to cook in it!

Well, first things first.

Where to Get Kitchen Stuff Cheap

Yard sales—great for all household stuff, but you do have to get up early. Really early.

Secondhand shops—excellent for small appliances like toasters, but make sure the equipment is in working order before you buy.

Discount or dollar stores—good for small items like vegetable peelers and measuring cups, but the products might be very crummy quality. It's depressing to have a utensil fall apart the first time you use it. Look the item over carefully before buying.

Restaurant supply stores—anything used in a restaurant has to be pretty sturdy, so the quality of the merchandise tends to be good. Things might cost a little more at first, but they'll probably last a long time.

Totally Essential Kitchen Stuff

You really need these:

- large frying pan (10 inches or 25 cm diameter) or larger
- small frying pan (6 inches or 15 cm diameter) or thereabouts
- large pot (6 quart/liter) or larger, *with* a lid
- small saucepan (2½ quart/liter)
- strainer or colander
- at least 2 mixing bowls— 1 large and 1 small
- microwave-safe casserole (2 to 3 quart/liter) with a lid

- small sharp paring knife
- large sharp knife
- wooden cutting board
- wooden spoon for cooking
- cookie sheet
- muffin pan
- measuring cup
- set of measuring spoons
- grater
- a couple of pot holders or oven mitts
- can opener

Very nice to have but not essential:

- a really big stock pot for making a huge vat of soup or spaghetti sauce
- collapsible vegetable steamer
- kitchen scissors
- roasting pan
- loaf pan
- pie pan
- soup ladle
- metal tongs
- vegetable peeler
- wire whisk
- blender
- electric mixer
- microwave oven
- food processor
- toaster
- rubber scraper
- metal spatula (lifter)
- wok
- garlic press
- potato masher

Kitchen Equipment You Don't Need

The following is a partial list of stuff you don't need. And there's plenty more where these came from. Who invents this junk, anyway?

- square egg maker
- garlic keeper
- duck press
- hamburger patty maker
- heart-shaped fried-egg mold
- spiral vegetable cutter
- string-bean slicer
- mushroom brush
- egg piercer
- happy-face toast embosser

So You Don't Have a Steamer

Steaming vegetables is a great way to cook them. It's better than boiling because you don't end up draining away all the flavor and vitamins, plus it's faster because you're only using a little bit of water. And a steamer basket—a cute little fold-up contraption that fits into the bottom of your pot—is an extremely cheap and worthwhile piece of kitchen equipment.

But you don't have one.

OK. So this is not a big problem. Do you have a strainer? A colander? Set this into a pot just big enough to hold the strainer suspended about 1 inch (2.5 cm) or so above the bottom. Fill with enough water to reach just below the strainer, dump in your vegetables, slam a lid on top (or cover with a makeshift hunk of foil), and bring to a boil. Watch the water level in the bottom of the pot, and add more if you need it.

Storing Food—What Should Go Where

You bought it, so now where do you keep it? Rule of thumb: when in doubt, keep it in the fridge. Except, of course, if it's frozen.

In the cupboard or pantry

- Flour
- Sugar
- Pasta, rice, grains, beans
- Canned foods
- Unopened jars of jam, mayonnaise, ketchup, pickles, salad dressing, stuff like that
- Vinegar
- Chocolate
- Spices and dried herbs
- Onions and garlic
- Potatoes
- Soup mixes
- Cookies, cake
- Nuts (can go in freezer for long storage)
- Vegetable or olive oil
- Bananas

In the fridge

- Eggs
- Cheese
- Dairy products
- Most fresh vegetables and fruit
- Meat, fish, poultry
- Opened jars of jam, mayonnaise, ketchup, pickles, salad dressing, stuff like that
- Cooked leftovers
- Bread, sometimes

In the freezer

- Ice cream
- Frozen foods, obviously
- Baked things—bread, cakes, cookies

Basic Kitchen Sanitation— A Life or Death Issue

You definitely don't want food poisoning. Definitely. Besides being totally disgusting, it can actually kill you, which is not a good thing. So, how do you avoid this experience? The following food-handling safety tips might help:

Don't thaw frozen foods on the kitchen counter. Bacteria grow quickly at room temperature, rapidly turning your hamburger into a

time bomb. Thaw them overnight in the refrigerator, or in the microwave just before cooking.

When in doubt, throw it out! Cooking meat that looks or smells weird doesn't make it safe to eat. Just get rid of it, and order a pizza instead.

Keep your work areas clean. This isn't just a Mom thing—this is a real safety thing. Wash your hands, cutting board, and utensils in hot, soapy water before and after messing around with food. Cross-contamination of food can happen when juices from raw meat or poultry come in contact with a surface (like a cutting board, a knife, or your hands) that then touches another food—such as bread or lettuce.

Forget the rare hamburger. Just forget about it. Cook ground beef, chicken, pork, and turkey until it is no longer pink, and fish until it flakes easily with a fork. And don't even *think* about eating any of that stuff raw.

Don't let cooked foods hang around at room temperature. Keep cold foods cold, and hot foods hot. And when you're done with that lasagna, stick it right into the fridge—don't leave it loitering on the counter.

Watch that potato salad! Keep all salads made with eggs or mayonnaise refrigerated until serving time. Going on a picnic? Use an oil and vinegar dressing instead of mayo. It would be embarrassing to poison Aunt Mildred.

The Care and Feeding of Your Refrigerator

It doesn't bark, doesn't slobber, doesn't ruin the furniture—a refrigerator is really better than a dog. Cooler than a cucumber, always ready for you with a snack or a cold drink, it makes ice cubes and Jell-O, and it doesn't ask much in return. What more could you possibly want from an appliance? The very least you owe it is a good home, and a little tender loving care.

Keep your refrigerator clean. Once a week or so, dig down to the bottom of the dreaded vegetable crisper and pull out all the stuff that has disintegrated—the rotten lettuce, the liquefied celery, the mushy tomatoes. Wipe out the drawer with clean paper toweling, and take a mental inventory of what needs to be used up immediately. Hunt through the shelves for leftovers on the verge of evolving into a new life form. Throw those out, and promise to eat the ones that have not yet begun to transmogrify. Toss a handful of baking soda into a small bucket of warm water and use this to wipe down the shelves.

Defrost the freezer regularly. For full details on this delightful job, see page 17. A clean, ice-free freezer helps the entire unit run more efficiently. And, besides, it will give you more room to store ice cream.

Store your leftovers in see-through containers. Being able to see what is in a container avoids the Disgusting Surprise Syndrome—you open a container, thinking it's blueberry yogurt and *yikes!* It's not. What is it? You can't remember. Save your recycled yogurt containers for keeping chocolate chips, mixing paint, and freezer storage.

Wipe up spills as soon as you notice them. No chemist has ever invented a glue with the sticking power of applesauce that has dried on a refrigerator shelf. No solvent known to man is capable of removing petrified fruit punch, desiccated egg white, or solidified spaghetti sauce. Don't wait until it's too late.

Keep your refrigerator between 34° and 40° F (2° and 5° C). If you're not sure, keep a fridge thermometer in a glass of water in the fridge to check. Or, less accurately, if the milk is cold without ice crystals, you're probably just about right. Most refrigerators have a dial somewhere inside that can be adjusted to control the temperature. Make *small* adjustments, leave the fridge overnight, and readjust, if necessary, in the morning.

A refrigerator works best when fully loaded, but not crowded. This might be difficult when you're broke, or when you have a houseful of voracious friends.

Cool food quickly before refrigerating. Putting a pot of boiling soup right into the fridge will cause the poor machine to work overtime. Instead, set the pot of soup (or whatever) into a bowl of ice water until it cools down a little, *then* refrigerate it.

Wrap smelly food tightly. The aroma of cat food, while it may be delightfully appealing to Fluffy, does nothing whatever to improve the flavor of chocolate cake. Likewise, Limburger cheese, onions, fried fish, and egg salad, to name just a few.

It's really true about baking soda. Keeping an open box in the fridge does help absorb odors. After a couple of months or so, replace the box with a fresh one. You can then use the old baking soda for cleaning the fridge, unplugging the drain, or deodorizing the cat's litter box. Don't, however, use it for baking.

Is your refrigerator running? (Well, you'd better go catch it …) If it's *not* running, first check to see that it's plugged in. Next, check that temperature control knob inside to make sure it hasn't been turned off. Finally, check the fusebox (do you know where it is?) for a blown fuse. When all else fails, call a professional repairman.

Defrosting the Freezer

This most dreaded of all kitchen jobs really doesn't deserve its bad reputation. We've all heard some horror story about a friend who punctured the lining of her freezer with a chisel, resulting in not only an outrageous repair bill but also contributing to the tragic destruction of the earth's ozone layer (possibly leading to the extinction of the Wooly Lousewort). But this doesn't have to happen to you.

There are basically two types of refrigerator freezers—the kind that has a smaller door inside your big refrigerator door, and the kind with a separate outside door altogether. Either type will, alas, require defrosting from time to time. (Unless, of course, it's a frost-free, in which case you can skip this section.) The kind with an entirely separate door is a little easier to cope with, but neither one is really such a big ordeal.

First of all, don't wait until your freezer is so frozen up that you can't fit anything bigger than a Popsicle into it. Not only does a heavy build-up of ice take up valuable room, but it also interferes with the actual operation of the unit. Next, remove everything from the freezer. If all you have in there are four ice cubes and a Popsicle, you're in luck. But if the freezer is full of food, you'll need to keep this stuff from thawing while you work. Do you have a Styrofoam cooler? Use it. Or line a cardboard box with blankets, put in the frozen food, and cover them with more blankets. Or—if it's winter—put everything outside.

Now, if your freezer has a separate control dial inside, turn it to "off." Sometimes this dial is hidden in the refrigerator part (behind the milk). Sometimes there is no separate freezer dial at all, in which case just turn whatever dial you do find to "off." Next, prop the door open and go do something else. A couple of towels laid on the floor of the freezer will help absorb some of the water so you don't end up with a flood. If the freezer is one that is inside the refrigerator door, it may leak down into the refrigerator section, so you'll want to take out the vegetable drawer on the bottom and anything else you don't want soaked. Try to keep these things cool so they don't spoil. After an hour or so, most of the ice should be melted and you're ready to wipe it dry and resume a normal life.

But let's say you don't have the patience for this sort of thing. Let's say you're in a big hurry, for some reason. Let's say you're just a hyper kind of person. You *can* rush this along a little. Just a little. Don't get out the chisel (oh please, if only for the sake of the Wooly Lousewort). Use your blow dryer instead. Plug it in, set it on high, aim, and thaw. Loosen the ice from the sides of the freezer with a plastic scraper or some other similar harmless tool.

There. You've done it, and lived to tell the tale.

Oh, don't forget to put your frozen food back in the freezer and turn it back on. And treat yourself to a new batch of ice cubes. You deserve it.

Cleaning Your Stove

Oh, gross. How did it get this bad? Why didn't you wipe up that spaghetti sauce before it petrified on the burner? Why did you let that vegetable soup solidify like that? And what are these crusty black blobs anyway? Now, what do you do? Do you just have to throw the whole stove out? Nah. Just take a deep breath, gather up all the cleaning supplies you own, and put on some rubber gloves. You can do this.

Electric stoves First, make absolutely sure all the stove elements are *turned off and are cold*. An element that has recently been used may still be very hot—so be careful. Next, gently pull on an element, opposite from where it plugs into the stove, and remove it. It will usually come out pretty easily, the way a plug comes out of a socket. Remove all the elements the same way. Never force or twist them—you're better off leaving an element in place if it seems really stuck. Set these aside.

Under each element, there will be a removable drip tray. Take these out and put them in the sink to soak in very hot water while you clean the top of the stove. Using a sponge and a nonabrasive cleaner, scrub the entire stovetop clean. Really stuck-on stuff may need a little extra encouragement—like a plastic scrubber. Never use steel-wool pads or scouring powder on an enamel stovetop. An old toothbrush is handy for getting into those disgusting little crevices filled with brown crud. Do the knobs come off? Good. Clean them too. Next, scrub the drip pans clean. For those, you can use steel wool pads, or whatever will work. Dry them and wrap them in aluminum foil—cheaper than ready-made disposable trays and not all that much work to do. Now, put the whole business back together, stand back, and admire your work.

Gas stoves Remove the grate from each burner and soak in a sinkful of hot water. Does your stove have removable drip pans under the burners? If it does, remove them and let them soak with the grates. Using a sponge and a nonabrasive cleaner, scrub the stovetop, and whatever parts you can easily get at. Use a toothbrush to get into those yucky spots. If the knobs come off, clean under them too. Don't pull out any pipes or tubes, and if the stove has a pilot light, make sure you don't accidentally blow it out. On some stoves you can get at the area underneath the burners where all the really horrible old stuff collects. If you can, then *do it*, even though it makes you sick. Finally, scrub the drip pans and the burner grates clean, and wrap the drip pans in aluminum foil. Put all the parts back where they came from, and relax. You're done.

The oven Yes, the oven. A scary place, if ever there was one. First, scrape up as much of the loose stuff as you possibly can, and get rid of it. A pancake turner works well for removing large clumps of cremated crud. Now, you may or may not be relieved to learn that commercial oven cleaner is really the way to go. It smells bad, burns your skin and, environmentally speaking, it's not nice stuff. But still, it works. And if you follow the directions on the container, you should be clean in no time. Sort of.

Prevention

- Wipe up spills as soon as possible—don't let them burn on.
- Place a sheet of heavy-duty aluminum foil on the bottom of the oven to catch overflows.

- Make sure your pot is big enough that the contents don't boil over.
- Use a spoon rest (really) to prevent sloppy messes on the stovetop.
- Don't cook. Eat out. Just kidding.

How to Unplug a Drain

You knew you shouldn't pour that grease down the drain, didn't you? And those cornflakes—don't tell me they were an accident. And what about the macaroni? Huh? Now you have a totally plugged sink, and you're really sorry, aren't you? Well, it's gross, but not terminal.

First, let's try the environmentally friendly method. Get out the old bathroom plunger (you *do* have a plunger, don't you?) and, positioning the suction cup over the drain, give it two or three serious plunges. Does the water go down? If it does, your next step is to pour a kettleful of boiling water down the drain to wash out whatever disgusting stuff might be left in the drain. If you're lucky, this will do the trick.

If this method doesn't work, you'll have to resort to the big guns. First, scoop all the standing water out of the sink. Following the directions on the package, *carefully* use commercial drain cleaner, remembering to store the container in a safe, dry place when you're finished. Once the drain is clear, run lots of hot water down to flush out all the gunk.

And finally, if all else fails, call a plumber. They cost lots of money, so you don't want to do this too often.

To prevent this sort of thing from happening again, about once a week scoop a couple of tablespoons of baking soda down the drain, followed by a quart of boiling water. And, for heaven's sake, next time feed the leftover macaroni to the dog.

How Not to Run the Dishwasher

The main problem with dishwashers is that they are operated by lunatics (not you, of course) who expect them to perform impossible feats. Having left the dishes sitting around the kitchen for several hours (or days, or months), these maniacs then load them into this poor, hapless machine without so much as a rinse. Petrified spaghetti, desiccated rice, the remains of last week's fried egg— substances so tough that you could use them to build nuclear fallout shelters—in they go! And guess what happens! That's right—nothing! What a surprise. With some good old stupidity, a touch of laziness, and a basic lack of common sense, you too can have dirty dishes— even if you do have a dishwasher.

Never rinse, scrape, or in any way remove leftover food from your dishes before loading them into the dishwasher. If at all possible, let the debris age for a day or two (or more) before washing, to allow the grime to harden sufficiently. Applesauce, if left to cure, is particularly tenacious and interesting.

Always load the dishes into the dishwasher in such a way as to make it impossible for the water to reach all the soiled surfaces. If you can possibly position a large bowl directly over the sprayer, this will cut off the water spray almost completely, ensuring a satisfyingly filthy result.

Never put in the recommended amount of dishwasher detergent. Skimping on detergent will not only save you money, but it will also prevent annoyingly clean dishes. Better yet—don't put any in at all!

Make sure the hot water isn't really all that hot. After all, if you use really hot water, it is possible that even *without* detergent some food scraps will be removed from the dishes.

Always fill your dishwasher with fossilized frying pans, baking pans crusty with burnt-on food (lasagna is especially nice), and casseroles black with cremated macaroni and cheese. And don't soak them, either.

Never check the wash settings on the machine before turning it on. With any luck, the dishwasher has been set to some weird cycle like Plate Warmer or Rinse and Hold.

Finally, if all else fails and despite all your efforts your dishes still come out clean, you may just have to wash them by hand. But don't do it right away. You don't want to take any chances on getting them clean.

Appliance Troubleshooting for the Complete Idiot

Detailed description of symptoms:

1. It doesn't work.

2. It doesn't work *right*.

3. It makes funny noises.

4. There's water all over the floor.

5. Smoke and flames are coming out of it.

Highly technical investigation of problem:

1. Is it plugged in?

2. Is the fuse blown? (Do you even *know* where your fuses are?)

3. Is the cord frayed, or damaged, or looking scary?

4. Is it switched on?

5. Is the water/gas/electricity turned off?

6. Did some moron go and change the settings?

7. Is it all gunked up? Do you suppose it could use a good cleaning?

8. Is the element burned out? Maybe?

Solution:

1. Plug it in.

2. Replace the fuse or reset the circuit breaker.

3. Switch it on.

4. Reset the dial.

5. Clean it out.

6. Get it fixed. Not by you.

7. Get a new one. Sorry.

Shopping

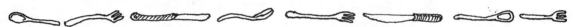

It's funny. You've been in a million supermarkets, you've picked up groceries before—this is nothing new. So then why do you fall apart the first time you go to buy a pound of hamburger? Or a green pepper? Or a bag of rice? How did shopping get so confusing?

For one thing, there's way too much stuff out there. There are too many choices. Everything is complicated. No matter what you want to buy, it comes in seven different flavors, five colors, and eight sizes. You can buy it wrapped in plastic, stuffed into a box, or loose in a bag. Do you want it frozen, fresh, or canned? Imported or domestic? Boneless? Precooked? Sliced? AAAAAAAGH!

OK. Calm down. Take a deep breath. You can do this.

Kitchen Staples

You're hungry. You're in the mood to cook something. You're not in the mood to go shopping. If you keep a supply of basics on hand, you'll always be able to whip something up.

- Flour
- Sugar
- Coffee and tea
- Salt
- Pepper
- Rice
- Vegetable oil
- Oatmeal
- Chocolate chips
- Canned beans
- Bouillon cubes or powder
- Pasta—something long (like spaghetti) and some kind of macaroni
- Canned tomatoes
- Canned tuna
- Spaghetti sauce
- Baking powder
- Baking soda
- Eggs
- Milk
- Onions
- Carrots
- Potatoes
- Garlic
- Bread
- Peanut butter
- Jam
- Cheese
- Apples
- Butter or margarine
- Cinnamon

Supermarket Strategies

Supermarkets are in the business of selling as much stuff as they possibly can. And they do it very well. When you go shopping, be aware of the booby traps that await an unsuspecting consumer—and avoid them.

Big rule: never shop hungry. Eat something *(anything)* before you set a single toe inside the supermarket or else you will find yourself buying things that you would normally be able to resist. If you don't think this is true, just try to walk down the bakery aisle without buying anything when you haven't eaten lunch.

Buy store brands. These are usually cheaper than name-brand products, and usually just as good. In fact, you might even like the store-brand potato chips or cookies better than your usual kind.

Buy big only when it makes sense. If it will take you a year to use up that humungous jar of jam, during which time it will go bad, then it doesn't make sense to buy it. On the other hand, if a five-pound bag of carrots costs just a few pennies more than a two-pound bag, go for it—just don't forget to eat them.

Beware the ends of the aisles. Don't assume that just because something is displayed at the end of an aisle, it's on sale. Sometimes it's not. Very sneaky. Check the price.

Buy only what you really need. Make a list at home and take it with you to the store. If you just need milk and a loaf of bread, go straight for those items, pay for them, and leave the store. Immediately. Do not walk past the cookies, and do not linger at the ice cream.

Don't buy three peppers if you only want one. Ask the produce person (nicely) to (please) remove one pepper from the package and price it individually for you.

Check the dates on perishable items. Dairy products like milk and yogurt, baked goods like bread and rolls, and many other perishable foods are stamped with a Best Before date. This just means what it says—the item is best before a certain date. It does *not* mean that it is automatically rotten the day after that date—but it might be. Always buy the item with the longest expiry date to get the freshest stock.

Don't even look at the junk around the checkout counter. This is where they put all the stuff that no one needs. They're counting on you to surrender to impulse and buy a chocolate bar, or a magazine, or a package of gum. You're being manipulated! You must resist!

How to Buy Fruits and Vegetables

It's a jungle out there! Step into the produce section of any supermarket and you're instantly overwhelmed. There are oranges and apples and grapes and bananas. There are onions and eggplants and tomatoes and seven kinds of lettuce. There is stuff you've never heard of, and stuff you don't know what to do with. So? What are you waiting for—an engraved invitation? Will a few words of wisdom help?

25

Fresh fruits and vegetables should look and smell fresh. They should be firm and shiny, with no rotten spots. This doesn't mean you can't use an apple with a bruise on it, or a slightly droopy string bean. But if you're paying for fresh stuff, examine it carefully to make sure it really is worth buying. If it isn't, get something else instead.

Whenever possible, buy what's in season. It will be inexpensive, locally grown, and good quality. Eat apples in the fall, oranges in the winter, asparagus in the spring, and peaches in the summer.

Buy locally grown fruits and vegetables. This, of course, does not apply to such things as bananas, unless you happen to live in Costa Rica. But try not to buy imported tomatoes in August, for instance, when the local ones are available. Ask questions.

Shop at farmers' markets whenever you can. It's hard not to get involved with your cauliflower when you've talked to the guy who grew it. And there's no better way to make sure the stuff is really fresh.

Don't buy more than you can possibly use. It's pointless buying a huge basket of fresh peaches if you won't be able to eat them all before they rot.

Check out the clearance bin! Sometimes there are wonderful bargains to be found. Lots of this stuff is perfect if you plan to eat it right away. This area is a haven for banana-bread bakers and soup lovers.

Buy brussels sprouts even if you think you hate them. Just once. Maybe you just hate them the way your mom cooked them. Maybe you'll *love* them the way you cook them. You'll never know unless you try. This also goes for squash.

Who cares what it is—just try it! No vegetable will kill you. Even if you eat something raw that ought to be cooked, or cook something better left raw. Even a raw potato, while it may be *unusual*, is not toxic. So don't be afraid of buying something unfamiliar just because you don't quite know what to do with it.

How to Buy Meat

Meat is scary. It comes with no cooking instructions, it all looks identical, and the same chunk of meat may have several different names. It's almost enough to turn a person into a vegetarian. Or maybe not.

Make friends with a butcher. Ask stupid questions: What is this? What do you do with it? Is it any good? Most butchers will be only too happy to share pearls of carnivorous wisdom with anyone who is interested. An especially enthusiastic butcher may even divulge his favorite secret recipe.

The hamburger dilemma. Regular ground beef, medium ground beef, lean ground beef, *extra-lean* ground beef—what's next? Super-regular? Medium-lean? Extra-super-medium-deluxe-lean? It all has to do with how much fat is in the meat. So here we go: In general, *regular ground beef* (25% fat) will be cheapest—use it when you're cooking something that you can drain the fat off before the rest of the ingredients are added (spaghetti sauce, chili, that sort of thing). *Medium ground beef* (15 to 20% fat) is a good compromise—cheaper than lean but less fat than regular. Use medium in meatballs, meat loaf, burgers. *Lean and extra-lean ground beef* (5 to 10% fat) tend to be more expensive. Nice to use for low-fat hamburgers, if you can afford it.

What about ground turkey, chicken, lamb, pork? Go ahead and try one of them instead of ground beef in any recipe. The taste and texture will be different, but it'll work—you may even like it better.

No, sausages are not made from ground-up rats. Meat regulations are extremely strict, so unless you buy sausages from Igor down the street who makes them in his basement, you can be pretty sure it's all good stuff.

Roasts can be intimidating. Most big hunks of meat look alike, more or less. But they aren't alike. Ask anyone who has ever tried to roast a piece of stewing beef. If you don't know what you want to make, buy what's on sale and ask the butcher (or your mom) how to cook it. Or else ask which cut to buy for the recipe you have in mind. Either way, it pays to do your homework.

Not all steaks are created equal. A select few can be slapped on the barbecue just the way they are. Others should be marinated before cooking. And still others should be saved for something stewy.

Rule of thumb, meatwise: the rear of the animal is more tender than the front, if you know your anatomy.

A Brief Compendium of Meat
or
Help! How do you cook this thing?

Stuff for the barbecue	Stuff to roast	Pot roast and stew
Beef rib and rib-eye steak	Beef rib roast	Beef short rib
Beef wing steak	Beef rump roast	Beef chuck
Beef T-bone steak	Beef sirloin tip roast	Beef blade
Beef sirloin steak	Lamb leg or shoulder	Beef brisket
Beef strip-loin steak	Pork loin or shoulder	Beef round
Any ground meat	Pork leg	Beef stewing meat
Hot dogs and sausages	Ham	Lamb shoulder
Lamb loin or shoulder chops	Chicken	Lamb stewing meat
Pork rib or loin chops	Turkey	Pork shoulder chops
Pork spare ribs	Duck	Chicken
Smoked ham slice		
Chicken		

Cheese Shopping—An Adventure

There are (approximately) seventeen zillion kinds of cheese in the world. So why do you always buy that flat, plastic-covered kind? Doesn't it bother you that they call it "cheese food"? Otherwise, what would you think it was? Why not take a chance and try a tiny sliver of some other kind of cheese? Hey, you might even like it.

A cheese store is a wonderful place. It's stinky, filled with weird and wonderful things, and often run by someone who really knows about cheese. Best of all, a good cheese store will let you taste before you buy—which is nice when you really don't know what you're doing. It's even nice when you *do* know what you're doing. Don't be afraid to sound like an idiot—tell the cheese person you're new at this. Say you want to try something different. Try a really stinky cheese, or a blue cheese, or a sharp cheese. If you're timid, ask for something mild. How will you ever know what you like unless you try it? Go ahead—be daring.

The following extremely incomplete list will give you a start on your cheese adventures. You're on your own from there.

For slicing in sandwiches:
Havarti, Monterey Jack, Muenster, brick, Cheddar, Colby, Edam, Emmenthal, Swiss, Jarlsberg, fontina, Gouda, provolone

For cooking and baking:
Mozzarella, Monterey Jack, Cheddar, Colby, Emmenthal, Swiss, Jarlsberg, fontina, Parmesan, Romano, Gruyère

On crackers for a snack or appetizer:
Brie, Camembert, Havarti, Muenster, Saint Paulin, Oka, Cheddar, Colby, Edam, Emmenthal, Swiss, Jarlsberg, Gouda, goat cheeses

In salads:
Feta, Cheddar, Parmesan, blue cheese, Roquefort

The Freezer Zone

What lurks behind the glass doors of your supermarket's freezer section? Well, almost everything, really.

The frozen food section of a supermarket is a minefield. You can, if you're careful, find plenty of stuff that's inexpensive, nutritious, and really convenient. Or else you can end up with lots of overpriced, over-processed junk. It depends.

Buy frozen foods that are as close to their original state as possible. This means frozen fish fillets are a good choice, and frozen precooked breaded fish fillets with marinara cheese sauce are not. Frozen peas are a good choice, and boil-in-the-bag frozen peas with French onion gravy are not. The less processing a frozen food has had to endure, the less junk will have been added to it, and the cheaper (and better) it will be.

Stay away—far away—from frozen dinners.   Sure, the trays are cute. And in ten minutes you've got a total meal. With dessert, even. But it's not worth it. The food in it is almost always overprocessed, overcooked, and overpriced. In a big hurry? Scramble an egg with some veggies, cut up a cucumber, and toast a bagel. Need dessert? Eat an apple.

What about frozen pizza? Well, it's cheaper than ordering in. And usually not too bad. OK, keep one in the freezer for an emergency. Other items that might be handy to have in your freezer are meat or chicken pies or lasagna. As a main dish, when it's been one of those days, it sure beats a bag of potato chips, anyway.

Learn to cook! Some things are so easy to make that it's crazy to buy them already prepared. Those frozen spicy chicken wings you just bought wouldn't have taken very long to make, and you'd have done a much better job. If you do say so yourself. The same goes for macaroni and cheese, burritos, meatballs, shepherd's pie.

Alternative Shopping

The supermarket isn't the only place to get food. It isn't even a particularly interesting place to get food. Branch out a little. Explore a Chinese grocery. Investigate your local farmers' market. Be daring—buy something you don't recognize from a street vendor. Shop on the edge.

Your Friend the Bulk Food Store

So you buy a jar of oregano. The oregano weighs 13 grams. The jar (the jar!) weighs 122 grams. Does this make sense? What are you buying, anyway—the jar or what's inside it?

Dried herbs and spices are notoriously overpackaged in supermarkets. Refill your empty jars or containers with herbs and spices from the local bulk food store, and you'll save money while you cut down on garbage.

Buy exactly the amount you need. Don't buy a 500 gram bag of walnuts when you really only want a handful. On the other hand, if you really go through the chocolate chips (and who doesn't), keep a big jar filled with them to avoid those emergency midnight trips to the corner convenience store.

Why use a box or bag when you'll just be dumping it as soon as you get home? It's just more garbage. Instead, bring your own containers to the store and refill them yourself.

It's cheaper to buy bulk. You'll save about 30% over the supermarket price on most items when you shop at a bulk food store. Pretty amazing, when you think about it.

International grocery stores

There are Chinese groceries, and Lebanese groceries, and Indian groceries. There are shops that sell Mexican foods, and others that sell Italian foods. Every city has a few stores (or sometimes entire neighborhoods) that carry products used in the cooking from a certain country or region. The shopkeepers are often delighted to share their culinary secrets—you may come away with a bagful of strange groceries, and a few interesting recipes to go with them. Ask questions—no one will think you're an idiot.

Farmers' markets

Four kinds of potatoes, six kinds of beans, three kinds of cucumbers—did you even know these things existed? There's the butter tart lady, and the organic chicken people, and the cheese guys. There are eggs (white, brown, *and blue*), apples, and ultra-hot horseradish. How can you resist buying a basket of peaches from the actual person who picked them? Get up early, hike out to your local farmers' market, and check out what's growing these days.

Street vendors

You never know what you'll find on the street. Sometimes it's a rack of watches, sometimes it's T-shirts, sometimes it's homemade Chinese dumplings. Street vendors set up shop whenever and wherever they can, they sell whatever they can sell, and it's always a surprise. Buy a basket of overripe bananas and go home and make banana bread. Or pick up a case of mangos ("Very good! Very sweet! Special price!") and eat mangos for a week. Did these things fall off a truck? Was there a shipwreck nearby? You'll never know for sure.

Convenience Foods—the Good, the Bad, and the Silly

What is all this stuff? Space food? Why does our hamburger need help? Was it in trouble? And why do we need powdered sauce for our noodles? What's going on here, anyway?

A good convenience food is one that provides a shortcut, so that we can easily do our own cooking, minus the really annoying parts. For instance, using bouillon powder or canned broth allows you to make a

The Good	The Bad	The Silly
Canned broths	Powdered cheese sauce mix	Salad dressing
Bouillon powder	Burger and tuna mix	Seasoned rice mixtures
Spaghetti sauce	Instant mashed potatoes	Cracker and cheese combos
Canned fruit	Frozen whipped topping	Pre-shredded cheese
Canned beans	Instant rice	Cake/muffin/brownie mix
Oh, OK, biscuit mix	Pasta and sauce packets	Salad kits

pot of potato soup without having to make the stock from scratch first—something you probably don't want to do all the time.

A bad convenience food not only takes away all the fun of cooking, but it also convinces us that we can't cook from scratch, and worst of all, tastes yucky. Many of them are entirely artificial and ridiculously overpriced. Take this stuff camping, if you must.

A silly convenience food is just plain pointless. It doesn't save you very much time, isn't all that convenient anyway, and is often stupidly overpackaged. When it takes ten minutes to whip up a batch of brownies from scratch, why on earth would you ever need a mix?

Those Scary Herbs and Spices

They're scary. There are too many of them. You never have the one you need. Just the mere mention of the word "coriander" causes your hands to shake (see, it's happening already). Never mind cardamom. AAAAAAGH!

OK, calm down. Deep dark secret time: *There is not a single recipe that won't work anyway, even if you leave out every single herb and spice.* Not that you *should* leave them out, but you *can*. It won't taste exactly the way it was intended, but it will still be edible. Furthermore, you can put in more or less of a herb than the recipe calls for, and even more shocking, you can add something else altogether, if you want to.

So go ahead, do something wild. Use cumin instead of caraway! Use oregano instead of coriander! Leave out the cinnamon! Double the curry powder!

And you didn't think you were the reckless type.

Bare bones spice collection

What can't you do without?
  Salt and pepper
What else?
  Basil
  Oregano
  Cinnamon
  Paprika
  Fresh garlic
  Fresh parsley
Want to add just a few more?
  Cayenne pepper
  Curry powder
  Ginger
  Cumin
  Thyme
  Vanilla

Buying Eggs

Eggs are eggs, right? Well, yes and no.

Despite what some people think, there is absolutely no difference in taste or nutritional value between brown eggs and white eggs. The color of the shell is determined by the type of chicken it came from—brown chickens can lay white eggs, and white chickens can lay brown eggs, and some chickens even lay blue eggs. But that's another story. So buy whatever color egg goes with your decor, and don't worry about it.

The price of a dozen eggs varies mainly according to size. In general, if there's no more than a seven-cent price difference between one size and the next, buy the larger eggs—they're a better deal. And keep in mind that most recipes assume that you'll be using large-size eggs.

Junk Food—Or Is It?

What is junk food, anyway? Is pizza bad? Or is it good? Are French fries junk? And what about gummi worms? How's a person to know?

Junk food is any food that doesn't contain enough nutrients to make it worth its weight in calories. Some don't contain *any* nutrients. Any food that's high in sugar or fat, with very little redeeming protein, vitamins, or fiber—like gummi worms, sorry—is probably junk. On the other hand, pizza—which *can* be pretty salty and high in fat—is still OK because it also happens to be loaded with cheese, and vegetables, and other good stuff like that.

Then there are the junk foods that are *pretending* to be good for you—like granola bars, and chewy fruit snacks. Many commercial granola bars are too high in sugar and fat to be a *really* nutritious snack. And the ones that are covered with chocolate are, basically, chocolate bars. Fruit snacks are candy. Period. If you want a treat, have one of these. If you want fruit, have actual fruit.

So what should you do?

Well, first, read the ingredients on the package. Ingredients are listed proportionately in descending order—there's most of the first one and least of the last. Is sugar the first thing on the list? Junk. If you really want some junk, have it and get it over with. Then eat good stuff for the rest of the day. You don't have to give up eating chocolate bars and cheesies completely in order to have a healthy diet. Just don't let junk food *be* your diet.

After all, you are what you eat. A scary thought, isn't it?

Cheap Eats—How to Buy Food and Eat Cheaply

You're hungry. You're broke. So? What you need is a strategy.

Learn to cook. It's your best defense against poverty. It's usually much much cheaper to cook stuff yourself, and it's almost always better. Plus, knowing how to cook well is extremely advantageous to a person's love life. Really.

Don't eat out. At least not often. That hamburger you just paid $2.50 for is worth about fifty cents, maybe. And it wouldn't have taken very long to make either.

Stay away from processed foods. You pay for every single thing that someone else does to your ingredients. Like when someone else shreds up the cheese for you, or cuts the lettuce up into little pieces in a bag. Figure out how much it costs compared to doing it yourself. And, really, do you *want* a total stranger chopping up *your* lettuce? I mean, it's so *personal.*

Cook a turkey. No kidding. Just before Thanksgiving and Christmas, turkeys are always on sale everywhere—the ones marked "utility" are the cheapest—and there's nothing wrong with them (it's usually just

missing a wing or something). Buy one and cook the whole thing. Eat it plain the first night, in sandwiches the next day, a casserole for dinner, chopped up in spaghetti sauce, stir-fried with rice, and make soup from what's left. Then you'll be happy not to have turkey again until they go on sale next time. Want to try? See page 91 for the recipe.

Eat beans. They're cheap, they're nutritious, and cowboys like them, so they must be good. Canned beans are the easiest, but if you want to get *really, really* cheap, go for cook-it-yourself dried beans. You'll feel very, um, pioneer. Bean cooking instructions are on page 138.

Eat less meat. Or none. Try going vegetarian or partly vegetarian. Skipping just one meat meal a week can make a difference in your grocery bill, and you won't even miss it. Much.

Cruise the markdown area of the supermarket. Every store has a shelf or basket full of stuff that has been ripped or bruised or is just a little past its prime. There's usually nothing wrong with these things. Avoid dented cans, though—the contents may be spoiled.

Buy big. I mean, when it makes sense. *And* when you have the money. Getting a ten- or twenty-pound bag of potatoes costs not all that much more than buying just a couple of pounds of potatoes at a time. And they keep for weeks. Months. Consider sharing the cost of a huge bag of something (flour, onions, carrots) with some friends.

Breakfast—A Cruel Joke

The trouble with breakfast is that it comes too early in the day to be really decent. But still. You do need to get up and get going. And you do need to have breakfast. So what are you going to do about it?

A good breakfast doesn't have to be bacon and eggs and toast and all that jazz. It can be a leftover slice of cold pizza. It can be a blender concoction that you guzzle on the way out the door. Or it can be a tortilla with stuff inside that you can eat on the bus.

And on the weekend, when you really feel like messing around in the kitchen, breakfast can be pancakes. From scratch. With maple syrup. And you can eat them at noon, for all anyone cares.

Oatmeal from Scratch

You don't have to buy expensive packets of pre-chewed oatmeal in order to have it for breakfast. Both of the following methods are fast, easy, cheap, and good.

1 cup (250 mL)	**cold water**
½ cup (125 mL)	**quick-cooking rolled oats (not instant)**

Stovetop method

In a small saucepan, combine the water and the oats and bring to a boil over medium heat. Cook, stirring, for 5 minutes, until thickened.

Serve drizzled with honey, sprinkled with brown sugar and cinnamon, swimming in maple syrup, glopped with strawberry jam, or drowned in milk.

That's it. Done.

One gooey, warm serving.

Microwave method

In a large microwave-safe bowl, mix together the water and the oats. Microwave on high power for 2 minutes, stir, then microwave for another 1 or 2 minutes, until no longer watery.

Can you believe this?

One serving.

How to Boil an Egg

You feel cruddy. You want an egg. With some toast. Cut into triangles. Just like when you were little. Go ahead, it'll make you feel better.

To make a boiled egg, take your egg and put it in a small saucepan with enough cold water to cover it completely. Bring the water to a boil over medium heat. As soon as it reaches the boiling point, cover the pan with the lid and *turn off the heat*. Now, start timing your egg from this point:

Runny egg—2½ minutes
Soft egg—3 minutes
Soft egg with no gooey spots—4 minutes
Hard-boiled egg—15 minutes

This method is guaranteed to give you a *perfectly* cooked egg that will not explode in the water. Eat it out of a nice little eggy cup with your favorite Donald Duck spoon, sprinkled with a little salt and pepper, while watching cartoons in your pajamas.

How to boil water

Fill pot with water.
Put on stove.
High heat.
Bring to a boil.
Serve.

Very Basic Scrambled Eggs

Some people scramble them slowly over low heat, others flash-scramble them until they're nearly petrified. Some people add milk; others don't. Feel free to develop your own personal Scrambling Style from this very basic recipe.

Frying pan method

2	eggs
1 tbsp (15 mL)	milk
2 tsp (10 mL)	butter

Crack the eggs into a small bowl, add the milk, and beat them with a fork just until the yolk and white are combined.

Melt the butter in a small frying pan over medium heat, and heat until it gets foamy. When the foam subsides, pour in the eggs. Stir constantly, with a fork or a wooden spoon, until the eggs are cooked the way you like them.

Microwave method

2	eggs
1 tbsp (15 mL)	milk
2 tsp (10 mL)	butter

Measure the butter into a small microwave-safe dish, and microwave it on high power for 30 to 45 seconds, until melted and hot.

Beat together the eggs and the milk, until well combined, and add to the melted butter in the dish. Cook on high power, stirring twice, for 1 to 1½ minutes.

To cook *four* eggs, double the ingredients and cook on high power for 2½ to 3 minutes.

A Perfect Flat Egg

Cooking a fried egg isn't rocket science, but it does take a little finesse. So pay attention.

To cook one perfect flat egg

Melt 1 tbsp (15 mL) of butter in a small frying pan over medium heat. Let it get foamy, and when the foam subsides, adjust the heat to low and *very carefully* crack in the egg. *Do not* attempt to drop the egg from a great height into the pan because the yolk will break, and you will no longer have a *perfect* egg. There will be some bubbling and splattering but not too much. If the egg seems to be going berserk in the pan, you have the heat up too high.

Let your egg cook over low heat until you begin to see bubbles rising up from the bottom of the yolk. Gently lift the edge of the white to see if it is slightly browned on the bottom. If you like your eggs sunny side up, then it's probably done. If the top is still too runny, cover the pan with a lid for a minute to let it set, then serve.

If you are an easy-over type of person: *very, very gently* lift the egg up with a pancake turner, and *carefully* flip it onto the other side. The big trick, again, is to avoid breaking the yolk. Let it cook for no more than 30 seconds.

Done. Perfect.

Next time, try cooking 2 at once!

How to Cook Bacon

In a skillet:

Lay as many slices as will fit into a *cold* skillet without overlapping them. (Well, they shouldn't overlap *too much* anyway.) Turn on the burner and cook over medium heat for 6 to 8 minutes, flipping the slices over often, until they're done the way you like—crisp or still a bit floppy. Drain slices on a paper towel-lined plate for a minute before serving.

In the microwave:

On a microwave roasting rack (if you have one) or in a microwave-safe baking dish, arrange up to 8 slices of bacon in 1 layer. *Really* don't overlap them. Cover with a single layer of paper towel. Microwave on high power, *approximately* 1 minute per strip of bacon. Turn the strips over and rearrange them halfway through the cooking time so that they cook evenly.

Egg-in-the-Hole

A religious breakfast for those mornings when you're feeling, um, holy.

	butter
1	slice of white or whole wheat bread
1	egg (the regular kind)

Butter the slice of bread generously on one side. Using a 2½-inch (6 cm) round cookie cutter or an overturned glass about the same diameter, cut a hole in the middle of the slice of bread. Eat the middle immediately or save it for later. Whatever.

Lay the holey bread slice in a small frying pan, buttered side down, and cook over medium heat until just lightly golden on the bottom. Remove it from the pan with a spatula. Now add 2 tsp (10 mL) of butter to the pan, spread it around as it melts, and return the bread to the pan, *uncooked side down*. Immediately break an egg into the hole. It should just fit without too much leakage out the sides or top. Try not to break the yolk.

Let the egg cook over low heat until the white has just turned opaque—about 2 minutes. Slide the spatula underneath, and flip the egg-in-the-hole over to cook the top for just a minute.

Ta da! Egg-in-the-hole for one.

French Toast

You can just imagine how French toast was invented, can't you? Leftover bread, an egg, a little milk. It just happened.

1	egg
2 tbsp (30 mL)	milk
2 slices	bread, any kind, stale or fresh
1 tbsp (15 mL)	vegetable oil

In a flattish bowl, beat together the egg with the milk. Dip the bread slices into this mixture, turning to coat both sides. Depending on the type of bread and size of the slices, there might be enough of this egg mixture to do 3 slices of bread. But maybe not.

Heat the oil in a small frying pan. Lay the bread slices in the pan and cook them over medium heat, turning once, until nicely golden brown on both sides.

Makes 1 serving, but feel free to double, triple, quadruple (etc.) this recipe.

Breakfast Burrito

Here's a great breakfast that you can eat while you're hunting for your other shoe, trying to find that library book that's due today, or even while you're running for the bus.

Warm a small flour tortilla in the microwave for 20 seconds, or wrapped in foil in a warm oven for about 10 minutes. Meanwhile, make some scrambled eggs—the regular, frying pan way, or in the microwave (see page 38).

Scoop the scrambled eggs onto the middle of the warm tortilla, top with some grated cheese, a spoonful of salsa (volcano-hot salsa is a real eye-opener first thing in the morning), some shredded lettuce, chopped onions, green pepper, *whatever*. Fold up the bottom, roll in the two sides (leaving the top open), and away you go.

Pancakes Not from a Box

Believe it or not, it is possible to make pancakes without a mix. And it's not even hard.

1¼ cups (300 mL)	flour
1 tbsp (15 mL)	sugar
1 tbsp (15 mL)	baking powder
1	egg
1 cup (250 mL)	milk
2 tbsp (30 mL)	vegetable oil

In a medium-size bowl, stir together the flour, sugar, and baking powder. In another bowl, beat together the egg, milk, and vegetable oil. Add the egg mixture to the flour mixture and stir just until combined—a few lumps don't matter.

Heat a well-oiled griddle or frying pan over medium heat, then pour in about ¼ cup (50 mL) of the batter, spreading it out evenly. If the batter is too thick to pour easily, add a little more milk to thin it. Allow pancake to cook on one side until bubbles appear on the top, then flip it over, and let the other side cook until golden.

Once you get good at this, you can cook 2 or 3 pancakes at a time.

Makes about 14 4-inch (10 cm) pancakes.

Making soured milk— and why you'd ever want to do such a thing

Some recipes call for sour milk (or butter-milk). This (an acid) is used in combination with baking soda (a base) to provide a fun chemical reaction (see page 172) that causes bubbles—useful for making baked things rise. Pasteurized milk, however, does not sour in a nice, friendly way, the way milk used to in the olden days. So, instead, you'll cheat. Measure 1 tbsp (15 mL) of vinegar into a mea-suring cup. Fill the cup to the 1 cup (250 mL) mark with milk, and stir. Let it sit for about 5 minutes before using. You can do this anytime you come across a recipe that calls for sour milk or buttermilk.

Whole-Wheat Buttermilk Pancakes

Eat these pancakes and you'll feel so healthy it's scary. If you don't want to feel that healthy, you can make them with white flour instead.

1¼ cups (300 mL)	whole-wheat flour
1 tbsp (15 mL)	sugar
1 tsp (5 mL)	baking powder
½ tsp (2 mL)	baking soda
1¼ cups (300 mL)	buttermilk (or soured milk—see sidebar)
2 tbsp (30 mL)	vegetable oil
1	egg

In a medium bowl, combine the flour, sugar, baking powder, and baking soda. In another bowl, stir together the buttermilk, oil, and egg. Pour the buttermilk mixture into the flour mixture and stir just until com-bined. Don't overbeat this batter because you'll deflate the fluffiness.

Heat a well-oiled griddle or frying pan over medium heat, then pour in about ¼ cup (50 mL) of the batter, spreading it out evenly. Allow pancake to cook on one side until bubbles appear on the top, then flip it over, and let the other side cook until golden. Remove from skillet and do it again!

Serve immediately, or keep them warm on a plate in a slightly warm oven until they're all finished.

Makes about 12 4-inch (10 cm) pancakes.

Breakfast Pizza for One

Okay, so you can't quite bring yourself to just order a pizza for breakfast (anyway, they don't deliver at 7:30 a.m.), and that cold slice from two days ago doesn't look so great anymore. Try this.

2 tsp (10 mL)	**butter**
2	**eggs**
¼ cup (50 mL)	**spaghetti sauce**
¼ cup (50 mL)	**shredded mozzarella cheese**
	***and:* pepperoni, mushrooms, anchovies (?)— the usual**

Melt the butter in a small frying pan over medium heat. In a small bowl, beat the eggs and pour into the hot pan. Let the eggs cook until the bottom is golden and the top is no longer completely runny. With a pancake turner, flip the eggs over in the pan, and right away spoon some spaghetti sauce onto the cooked side, sprinkle with mozzarella cheese (and whatever else you're using), and cover the pan with a lid (or something—a plate will do). Let it cook for just 1 or 2 minutes, until the cheese melts.

Slide the pizza onto a plate, cut into wedges, and eat.

Breakfast in a Glass

You've overslept. Again. If you're not out of the house in two minutes, you're in big trouble. What about breakfast? Here—drink this and run.

1 cup (250 mL)	**cold milk**
1	**egg**
3 tbsp (45 mL)	**undiluted orange juice concentrate**
½	**medium banana**

Throw everything into the blender and let it zip while you tie your shoelaces.

Quick—into a glass—guzzle it down—and get going!

Beside the Point—Salads, Soups, Side Things

🍓 🍐 🍇 🍅 🧄 🥗 🥒 🌶 🌾 🥖 🥯 🍞 🍄 🌱 🧅 🫑 🦷 🥬 🥒 🐚 🦪

How to Make a Spectacular Salad

A salad is not just mere food, it is art. It is a philosophical statement. It is deep. It tells the world that you are sensitive, spontaneous, and slightly reckless. It will do wonders for your social life. The following is not a recipe.

Begin with some *greens*. Fill your bowl half full of the wildest assortment of green stuff you can get your hands on. Although *iceberg lettuce* is the stuff most people have in the fridge, it's not all that exciting. Try mixing it with some dark green *romaine*, some tender *Boston lettuce*, and some frilly *leaf lettuce*—red is nice. Add some *spinach*. Throw in some spicy *watercress* if you can find it, or some bitter *endive* leaves. Explore the leafy section of the supermarket for new colors, textures, and tastes. Be brave—*experiment*. Remember, you're spontaneous and reckless. Wash and dry the greens carefully, then tear them all up into bite-size chunks *with your bare hands*.

Now the accessories: *tomato* chunks, *cucumber* slices, chopped *scallions* or *red onion*, slivered red, green, or yellow *peppers*, *broccoli* or *cauliflower* chunks, thinly sliced *carrots*, shredded *red cabbage*, sliced raw *mushrooms*, *celery*, *radishes*, *bean sprouts*. Rummage through the vegetable bin of your fridge for inspiration. Throw in just enough of a few of these items to add color and flavor, without overloading the greens. Toss your salad together, and then add the finishing touches.

Stand back from your salad and give it the old hairy eyeball. Does it need some *cheese*? A little shredded *cheddar*, perhaps? Or maybe some chunks of *feta*? How about a few *olives*, or some chopped *apples* or *oranges*, or a handful of *peanuts*? This is your chance to be really daring. If you have access to a garden, add some *nasturtium flowers*, or some *pansies* (really—you can eat them), or *chive blossoms*. But not too much. Be restrained, yet unpredictable. Don't add any flowers you can't identify—some are poisonous.

Toss this creation together with a delicious homemade dressing (see page 47), serve to your adoring public, and please, try to be modest about it.

Cole Slaw

The world's cheapest and easiest salad. One head of cabbage makes a ton of cole slaw, and if you use the non-creamy dressing, it even improves with age. Creamy cole slaw should be eaten immediately.

½	small head of cabbage, shredded (about 6 cups [1500 mL])
1	carrot, grated
1	green pepper, chopped
2	green onions, chopped
1	apple, chopped (optional)
½ cup (125 mL)	raisins (optional)

Combine all the shredded and chopped vegetables (etc.) in a large bowl. Toss with either of the cole slaw dressings (pages 49–50). If you've added the apple and raisins to your cole slaw, it will go especially well with the creamy dressing. Otherwise use the non-creamy dressing.

How to chop an onion without crying

Amaze your friends and family with this spectacular trick! Take your cutting board and place it on the **front** burner of the stove. Now pay attention here—**this is critical**—turn the **back** burner on high. *The back burner.* Got that? Put your onion on the cutting board on the *front* burner and chop away to your heart's content. Due to complex scientific reasons, the heat from the back burner of the stove attracts the tear-producing onion vapors, drawing them away from your delicate eyeballs. Unbelievable, but true. Just *please* don't forget to turn that stove burner off when you're finished chopping. And, of course, take a bow. TA DA!

How to chop any vegetable

Obviously, vegetables don't want to be chopped. Or so it would seem. In a pathetic attempt to avoid being minced, vegetables are very inconveniently shaped. They have round sides. They have uneven bumps. They have seeds. But, alas, these strategies cannot save them from our superior intellect!

Onions

Round, firm vegetables like potatoes, eggplant, squashes, turnip

Long vegetables like carrots, zucchini, cucumbers, celery

Leafy vegetables like cabbage, lettuce

Peppers

Broccoli and cauliflower

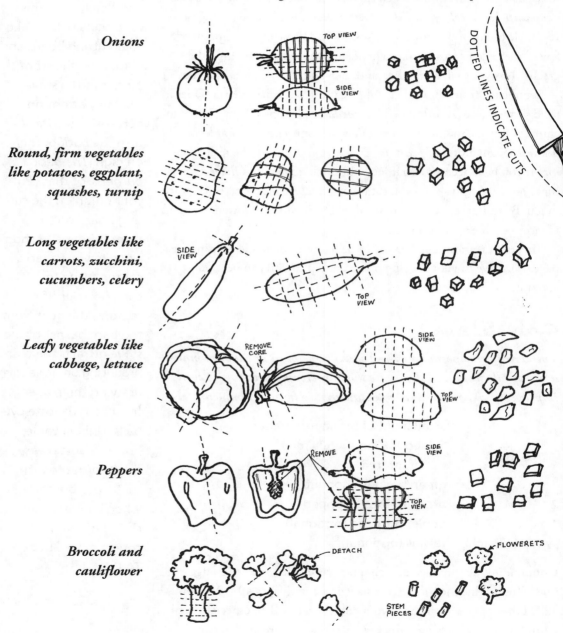

How to Make Some Spectacular Salad Dressings

You can (and should) make your own salad dressing. It costs next to nothing, takes about five minutes to do, and will be better tasting and fresher than anything you can buy in a store.

Basic Vinaigrette Dressing

This is a no-nonsense dressing that can be used as is, or it can be the start of some more elaborate concoction. Use any kind of oil you like, and whatever vinegar you happen to have. Experiment with different oils and vinegars (or try lemon juice instead), add herbs, spices, grated cheese, garlic, ketchup, mustard—mess around with this and see what you come up with.

½ cup (125 mL)	olive (or other) oil
¼ cup (50 mL)	vinegar
	salt and pepper

In a small bowl, whisk the ingredients together until thoroughly mixed, or put them in a jar and shake with the lid on.

Makes about ¾ cup (175 mL) of dressing—enough for a large salad, but leftovers can be kept in the fridge practically forever. The oil may thicken when it's chilled, but it will reliquefy at room temperature.

Creamy Italian Dressing

Start with a batch of Basic Vinaigrette dressing, then add some stuff and turn it into Creamy Italian. Just like that.

1 recipe	Basic Vinaigrette Dressing (see above)
3 tbsp (45 mL)	mayonnaise
1	clove garlic, squished
½ tsp (2 mL)	oregano
½ tsp (2 mL)	basil
	salt and pepper

In a small bowl, whisk the ingredients together until thoroughly mixed.

Makes nearly 1 cup (250 mL) of dressing—enough for a large salad. Leftovers can be kept in the fridge for a week.

Slightly Caesar Dressing

Another Vinaigrette variation. See, isn't it useful?

1 recipe	**Basic Vinaigrette Dressing (see page 47)**
3 tbsp (45 mL)	**mayonnaise**
1	**clove garlic (or more), squished**
1 tsp (5 mL)	**Dijon mustard**
2 tsp (10 mL)	**Worcestershire sauce**
1 tbsp (15 mL)	**grated Parmesan cheese**
1 tbsp (15 mL)	**minced canned anchovies (a classic touch, but optional)**
	salt and pepper

Whisk together the vinaigrette dressing and mayonnaise until well mixed. Add the garlic, mustard, Worcestershire sauce, Parmesan cheese, and anchovies to the vinaigrette dressing and whisk until smooth. Taste, and add salt and pepper, if you think it's needed.

Makes a little more than 1 cup (250 mL) of dressing. Leftovers can be refrigerated for 2 or 3 days.

What Is a Garlic Clove, and How Do You Chop It?

When a recipe calls for a clove of garlic, it means one *section* of the bulb. If the recipe calls for a head of garlic (we're talking *serious* garlic here) you'll be using the *whole bulb*.

Some recipes ask you to *chop*, *mince*, or *squish* a clove of garlic. Here's a quick, violent method to do it: place the clove on a chopping board, yell "HAYAH!" and whack the garlic firmly with the side of a broad knife or cleaver. The skin will peel off, and the garlic clove will be mostly in pieces. Remove the bits of skin. A few additional chops and you're done. Very effective.

Desperation Ranch Dressing

Desperation can be the mother of invention.

| ½ cup (125 mL) | mayonnaise |
| ¼ cup (50 mL) | pickle juice (any kind) |

Mix together the mayonnaise and the pickle juice, adjusting the seasoning, if necessary, until it tastes right. You can use the juice from any kind of pickle for this, but dill pickle juice is recommended by the experts.

Makes ¾ cup (175 mL) of dressing—enough for a couple of big salads. Leftovers keep well.

Zorba the Greek Dressing

½ cup (125 mL)	olive oil
¼ cup (50 mL)	lemon juice
1 tsp (5 mL)	oregano
	salt and pepper

Whisk together all the ingredients until combined.

Use this dressing on a romaine lettuce salad, with some tomato, black or kalamata olives, red onion, and crumbled feta cheese.

Makes ¾ cup (175 mL) of dressing—enough for a large Greek salad. You can keep the leftover dressing in the fridge for about a week.

Creamy Cole Slaw Dressing

½ cup (125 mL)	mayonnaise
½ cup (125 mL)	plain yogurt
	salt, pepper, and a pinch of sugar (if you want)

In a small bowl, mix together the mayonnaise and yogurt until creamy. Season with salt, pepper, and a pinch of sugar if it's too tart for your delicate taste buds.

Makes 1 cup (250 mL) of dressing—enough for a very large bowl of cole slaw. Leftovers don't keep very well, so only make as much as you can use right away.

Not-Creamy Cole Slaw Dressing

¼ cup (50 mL)	vegetable oil
¼ cup (50 mL)	vinegar
½ tsp (2 mL)	sugar
1 tsp (5 mL)	celery seeds or caraway seeds (if you have any)
	salt and pepper

Whisk all the ingredients together in a small bowl.

Makes about ½ cup (125 mL) of dressing—enough for a medium bowl of cole slaw. This type of salad will keep very nicely for several days, refrigerated, and is actually better the next day.

The Best Potato Salad

Even better than your mom's. But don't tell her that.

4 or 5	medium potatoes, scrubbed but not peeled
2 tbsp (30 mL)	vinegar
2 tbsp (30 mL)	water
½ tsp (2 mL)	salt
¼ tsp (1 mL)	pepper
1	small onion, chopped
1	stalk celery, diced
1 or 2	hard-boiled eggs, peeled and chopped
2 tbsp (30 mL)	chopped fresh parsley
½ cup (125 mL)	mayonnaise

In a medium saucepan, cover the potatoes with water and boil until tender but not mushy. Or, if you prefer, steam them in a steamer basket over boiling water. Depending on the type and size of potato, this could take 20 to 35 minutes. To tell if it's cooked, poke a knife into a potato—it should slide right in without hitting a hard spot. Drain, and let the potatoes cool just until you can handle them easily.

Peel the potatoes (they should practically peel themselves) and cut them into ½-inch (1 cm) cubes. Mix together the vinegar, water, salt, and pepper and toss with the potato cubes, being careful not to mush them up. Refrigerate until completely cool.

Add all the rest of the ingredients—the onion, celery, eggs, parsley, and mayonnaise—and toss until everything is well mixed. Chill thoroughly.

Makes 3 or 4 servings.

Cucumber Salad

When lettuce is $2 a head, and tomatoes are as tough as tennis balls, you can still have a salad with dinner.

½ cup (125 mL)	white vinegar
½ cup (125 mL)	water
1 tbsp (15 mL)	sugar
2	large cucumbers, peeled and thinly sliced (about 3 cups/750 mL)
	salt and pepper

In a medium bowl, combine the vinegar, water, and sugar. Add the cucumber slices to the dressing, toss, and refrigerate until serving time.

When you're ready to eat, drain the cucumber slices into a bowl, sprinkle with salt and pepper, and a little chopped dill (or dried), if you have it.

Makes 3 or 4 servings.

Chunky Pasta Salad

Pasta salad was invented to take care of leftovers. A bit of pasta, some shreds of pepper, a few cooked green beans, half an onion, a forgotten hunk of cheese—that sort of thing. Throw it all into a bowl with some dressing and you've made something out of nothing.

2 cups (500 mL)	*raw* rotini (or other large-ish) pasta—or 3 cups (750 mL) any *cooked* leftover pasta
1 tsp (5 mL)	vegetable oil
3 cups (750 mL)	mixed diced cooked and raw vegetables, cheese, ham, cooked chicken, salami, canned chick peas or beans—whatever you like
2 tbsp (30 mL)	chopped fresh parsley
¼ cup (50 mL)	mayonnaise
¼ cup (50 mL)	plain yogurt
2 tsp (10 mL)	cider (or plain) vinegar
¼ tsp (1 mL)	garlic powder
	salt to taste

If you're making the pasta especially for this occasion, cook it until it is still just a bit chewy, then drain it, and rinse under cold running water.

Toss with the vegetable oil to help keep it from sticking together. If you're using leftover pasta, rinse with cold water to revive it, then toss with oil.

In a large bowl, mix together the pasta, all the vegetables, the chicken, cheese (or whatever you have), and the chopped parsley. Cover with plastic wrap and refrigerate until serving time.

In a small bowl, whisk together the mayonnaise, yogurt, vinegar, garlic powder, and salt. *Just before serving*, pour over the salad, and toss well to coat everything with dressing. Don't add the dressing too far ahead of time, because the pasta will soak it up like a sponge. Taste, and adjust the seasoning the way you like it.

Any leftover salad may need another shot of dressing to rejuvenate it. Makes 3 servings. Or so.

Antipasto

Antipasto is a work of art. A symphony. Well, maybe that's a little much. But anyway, it's not meat loaf. Although there could be meat loaf in it. Or practically anything else, for that matter. It can consist of three or four well-chosen things arranged on a plate, or it can be a wild collection of odds and ends. It can be an appetizer, or it can be dinner. And the nicest thing about it is that you don't actually have to cook anything.

Some of the following items can be found at an Italian grocery, some can be picked up from your supermarket deli, and some of these things come out of cans or jars. Use your imagination—*express yourself* in your antipasto:

- marinated artichoke hearts
- sliced provolone cheese
- anchovies
- olives—green, black, wrinkled, spicy, stuffed, unstuffed
- thinly sliced Italian salami or ham
- canned sardines
- pickled peppers
- marinated mushrooms
- cherry tomatoes or tomato wedges
- roasted peppers or eggplant
- tuna
- sardines
- hard-boiled egg wedges
- celery and carrot sticks

Arrange your chosen antipasto components decoratively on a platter—rolling up the cheese and salami, making a face with the olives, garnishing everything with a pickled pepper—you know the sort of thing—and serve with a warm loaf of crusty Italian bread.

Potato Soup

Hey, a loaf of bread, a big bowl of potato soup—what more do you need? OK, maybe a car.

2	medium onions, chopped
2	cloves garlic, squished
2 tbsp (30 mL)	butter, margarine, or vegetable oil
4	large potatoes, cubed
4 cups (1 L)	water
4 tsp (20 mL)	instant chicken or vegetable bouillon powder (or 4 cubes)
2 cups (500 mL)	milk
	salt and pepper

In a large pot, sauté the onions and garlic in the butter or oil for a couple of minutes, just until softened. Add the potatoes and the water and bouillon powder or cubes. Bring to a boil over medium heat, then cover and simmer 15 to 20 minutes, until the potatoes are squishy.

Now, if you want a smooth soup, pour this mixture into a blender or food processor (you may need to do it in batches), then return the soup to the pot and add the milk. Otherwise, you can just mash the potato cubes up a bit with a fork, and add the milk. The blended version is slightly more elegant, but either way it's delicious. Heat the soup through, without boiling, season with salt and pepper, and serve.

Makes 4 to 6 servings.

Pumpkin Soup

There are few sights more pathetic than a shriveled old pumpkin the day after Halloween. Don't allow your jack-o'-lantern to die in vain. Make this soup.

1	onion, chopped
2 tbsp (30 mL)	butter
4 cups (1 L)	peeled, cubed, raw pumpkin
2	medium potatoes, peeled and cubed
4 cups (1 L)	chicken broth (canned, or from bouillon powder or cubes)
	salt, pepper, and (maybe a pinch of) curry powder

In a medium saucepan, sauté the onion in the butter for about 5 minutes, until soft. Add the pumpkin and the potato, and stir around for a minute or so. Pour in the chicken broth, cover, and let the mixture simmer until the pumpkin and potato are really soft—about 30 minutes.

Purée the whole business in a blender or a food processor until smooth, or just mash it up with a potato masher. The masher method is a little less elegant, but just as tasty. Return the soup to the pot to reheat, adding a little more broth or a splash of milk if it seems too thick. Season with salt and pepper (and a little curry powder, if you're the type), and serve.

Makes 4 to 6 servings.

Spinach Soup

Sometimes you just need something green.

2 pkgs	fresh spinach (10 oz/285 g each)
4 cups (1 L)	milk
2 tbsp (30 mL)	butter
1	small onion, finely chopped
2 tbsp (30 mL)	flour
	salt, pepper, nutmeg

Rinse the spinach under running water, break off the stems, pick out the weird wilted bits and anything that doesn't look like spinach, and dump the spinach into a pot. Pack the spinach down into the pot so that it all fits. Don't add any more water than what's left clinging to the leaves from washing. Cover with a lid and cook over medium heat, stirring from time to time, until the spinach has completely wilted and shrunk into a sorry-looking mass in the bottom of the pot. Dump the spinach and all its liquid into a blender, add 2 cups (500 mL) of the milk, and blend until smooth.

In the same pot, melt the butter and sauté the onion over medium heat just until soft—about 5 minutes. Add the flour, stir well, then pour in the remaining 2 cups (500 mL) of the milk. Gently bring this just to a simmer, stirring, until the soup thickens slightly, then pour in the blended spinach mixture and allow to just heat through (don't let it boil). Season with salt and pepper, and sprinkle each serving with a little nutmeg (if you like that sort of thing).

Makes 5 to 6 servings.

X-ray Vision Soup

This soup is so full of carrots that after you eat a bowlful, you'll be able to see right through walls. Not to mention clothing. Lead-lined underwear is recommended for bashful eaters.

2 tbsp (30 mL)	butter
1	onion, chopped
3 cups (750 mL)	peeled, coarsely shredded carrots
¼ tsp (1 mL)	turmeric (if you have it)
4 cups (1 L)	chicken broth
½ tsp (2 mL)	Italian seasoning (or dried oregano, thyme, basil, or dill)
1 cup (250 mL)	corn kernels (fresh, frozen, or canned)

Melt the butter in a large saucepan and sauté the chopped onions over medium heat until softened—about 5 minutes. Add the shredded carrots and the turmeric, and cook, stirring, until wilted. The turmeric will give the soup a super-bright yellow color, but if you don't have any, just leave it out.

Add the chicken broth and Italian seasoning, bring to a boil, and simmer for 10 minutes. Add the corn, and cook for another 5 minutes or so. Taste and adjust the seasoning with salt and pepper, if you think it's necessary.

Makes 6 to 8 servings.

Multibean Soup

Go ahead—mess around with this recipe. Change the beans to match your decor, add or subtract vegetables, rearrange the seasonings. It's your soup—have your way with it.

½ cup (125 mL)	split peas
¼ cup (50 mL)	dried red kidney beans
¼ cup (50 mL)	dried lima beans
¼ cup (50 mL)	dried pinto beans
¼ cup (50 mL)	dried chick peas
6 cups (1.5 L)	water
2 tbsp (30 mL)	vegetable oil
1	onion, chopped
1	green pepper, chopped
1	stalk celery, chopped
1	carrot, chopped
1	clove garlic, squished
5 cups (1.25 L)	water
¼ tsp (1 mL)	dried basil
4 tsp (20 mL)	beef or vegetable bouillon powder, or 4 bouillon cubes
1 cup (250 mL)	chopped tomato
¼ cup (50 mL)	ketchup

In a large pot, combine the split peas and all the beans. Sort through them carefully, and remove anything unbeanlike, such as small stones, or loose coins, or whatever. Rinse them very well with cold water, and drain.

Add the 6 cups (1.5 litres) of water to the pot, bring it to a boil over medium heat, and let it boil for 2 minutes. Remove from heat, and let the pot sit, covered, for at least 1 hour. Go do something useful, like clean your room. (This is a quick soaking method for the beans that partly rehydrates them before cooking.)

When you return to the beans, they will be ready to *really* get cooked. Bring them to a boil again, over medium heat, and cook for about 1½ hours, until the beans are tender.

Meanwhile (and you have lots of time here), you can chop all the vegetables. Heat the oil in a medium-size pot, add the chopped onion, green pepper, celery, carrot, and garlic, and sauté for a couple of minutes. Pour in the 5 cups of water, and let simmer for 20 minutes, until almost tender.

When the beans are done, drain off their cooking liquid, and add the sautéed veggies and their liquid to the multibeans. Also add the basil, the bouillon powder, the chopped tomato, and the ketchup. Simmer this for about ½ hour or so. Season to taste with salt and pepper.

Makes at least 8 servings of good old rib-sticking soup.

Turkey Carcass Soup

It does sound sort of disgusting, doesn't it? It's not.

1	turkey carcass—the naked bones of a roast turkey (plus any leftover skin, gravy, meat scraps, etc.)
10 cups (2.5 L)	cold water
2	carrots, peeled and sliced
1	medium onion, chopped
2	stalks celery, sliced
	salt and pepper
1 cup (250 mL)	uncooked medium-width noodles

By hand, break up the turkey carcass into manageable hunks. Add the water and the vegetables, and bring to a boil. Cover, reduce heat, and let this concoction simmer for 1 to 1½ hours. Taste broth, and adjust seasoning.

Strain the broth and discard the bones, but keep the vegetables. Return the veggies to the broth, along with any bits of leftover turkey and/or gravy you might have lying around in the fridge. Add the uncooked noodles, bring to a boil, and cook just until the noodles are done.

Makes 4 to 6 servings.

Chicken Soup

It started as a scratchy throat. Then you got a stuffy nose and a headache. And now you're coughing. Make some chicken soup, wrap yourself in a blankie, and eat it in front of the TV. Maybe that "Star Trek" with the tribbles will be on again.

5 lbs (2.5 kg)	chicken necks and backs (or whatever's really cheap)
1	large onion
4	stalks celery, cut into chunks
4	large carrots, cut into chunks
3	cloves garlic, peeled but left whole
1 handful	fresh parsley, if you have it
8 cups (2 L)	cold water
1 tbsp (15 mL)	salt
1 tsp (5 mL)	pepper

Rinse the chicken pieces under running water and put them into your biggest pot. Add the onion, celery, carrots, garlic, and parsley, and pour in the cold water. The water should cover all the stuff in the pot with about an inch (2 cm) or so to spare. If it doesn't, add a bit more water. Bring to a boil over medium heat, then lower the heat so that the soup just simmers. Cook it, partly covered with a lid, for at least 2 hours.

Add the salt and pepper after the soup has been cooking for about an hour. At the end of the cooking time, taste it, and adjust the seasoning. If you have a cold—remember, your taste buds are shot—have someone else taste it for you.

Strain the soup into another pot, then skim as much of the fat (the clear, yellowish, floaty stuff) off the top as possible and discard it. (Neat trick: if you're not in a big hurry for your soup, refrigerate the broth overnight, then you can just scoop the congealed fat off the top easily.) Pick any meat off the bones, and cut up the carrots and the celery to add to the broth. If you want noodles (and who wouldn't?) cook them separately in boiling water before adding them to the chicken soup.

There you go. This will make you feel *much* better.

This chicken soup can also be consumed by a perfectly healthy person.

Minestrone Soup

Old Italian Minestrone Soup Secret: if you grate your own Parmesan cheese, save the rinds, and toss a couple of hunks into the soup with the tomatoes. Fish them out of the pot before serving.

¼ cup (50 mL)	olive or vegetable oil
2	medium onions, chopped
2	cloves garlic, squished
1	carrot, sliced
2	stalks celery, sliced
1 28-oz (796 mL)	can tomatoes, broken up
4 cups (1 L)	water
½ cup (125 mL)	any small pasta, uncooked (like little shells or alphabets)
1 cup (250 mL)	sliced green beans
2	small zucchini, sliced
3 cups (750 mL)	raw spinach, shredded
1 19-oz (540 mL)	can kidney (or other) beans

Before you do anything else, chop, dice, and slice everything that will need to be chopped, sliced, and diced for the soup. You'll be glad you did.

Heat the oil in a large pot and sauté the onions and garlic for about 5 minutes, until softened. Add the carrot, celery, tomatoes with all their juice, and the water, and bring to a boil over medium heat. Reduce the heat, cover, and simmer for about 40 minutes, or just long enough to clean up the mess in the kitchen. Almost.

Now, add the pasta and the green beans, and cook for 10 minutes. Finally, add the zucchini, spinach, and canned beans, and cook for another 10 to 20 minutes. Season to taste with salt and pepper, and serve sprinkled with grated Parmesan cheese.

Makes about 10 servings.

How to Make a Great Sandwich

Oh sure, you can slap a slice of baloney between two slices of white bread and call it a sandwich. And technically, it is. But is it a great sandwich? Not likely. A great sandwich is a creation. It is a thing of beauty. And besides, it goes so well with a bowl of soup.

1. The bread is the main thing. It should be fresh, and have *character*. Look for whole-grain bread, crusty bread, bread with cheese in it. Whatever. Slightly stale bread can work if you toast it.
2. The filling. Rummage through the fridge to find a forgotten treasure. A single lonely piece of leftover chicken. Cold meat loaf. Some stinky cheese. A hard-cooked egg. Baked beans. Avoid anything green and furry.
3. Accessories. Lettuce, tomato, onion, hot peppers, alfalfa sprouts. What about some olives? Or leftover cole slaw? Pickles? Anchovies? Don't be shy—it's only a sandwich.
4. The assembly. First, waterproof the bread. Butter works nicely, but so does mayonnaise. How about a mixture of mayonnaise and mustard? Or cheese spread, or hamburger relish, or peanut butter, or barbecue sauce. There has to be *something* interesting in the fridge. Next, layer on your filling ingredients and accessories. Make up a totally weird combination and see how it tastes. Elvis liked peanut butter and onion with mayonnaise. Yum.
5. Slam on the top, cut it in half (diagonally? in quarters? squares?), and after taking a moment to admire your creation, *eat it*.
6. Elvis would be proud.

Onion Soup au Gratin

You are sitting in a leetle bistro, weeth a très spéciale personne. Ze garçon brings you la soupe. You mange. Très romantique, n'est-ce pas?

3	onions, thinly sliced
2 tbsp (30 mL)	butter
6 cups (1.5 L)	beef broth (reconstituted canned is fine)
4	thick slices French or Italian bread, toasted
1 cup (250 mL)	grated Swiss or mozzarella cheese

In a medium saucepan, s-l-o-w-l-y sauté the sliced onions in the butter until golden brown. This will take longer than you'd expect—maybe 30 minutes or so. Don't try to rush it. Add the beef broth and simmer, covered, for about 20 minutes. Add salt and pepper—but go easy because canned broth tends to be pretty salty already.

Ladle the soup into 4 ovenproof bowls. Float a slice of toasted bread in each one, and sprinkle evenly with the grated cheese. Put the bowls onto a baking sheet, turn the oven to *broil*, and cook for a couple of minutes, until the cheese melts and gets bubbly.

Unfortunately, this serves 4, so you'll have to invite another couple.

Pita Pockets

Pita bread is a wonderful thing. There is almost nothing that can't be stuffed into it. Rummage through the refrigerator to find odds and ends of leftovers, bits of lettuce, tomato, cheese, a few shreds of chicken. None of these is enough to really make a meal out of, but together they are transcendent (look it up).

Begin with a very fresh pita bread. Stale pita will crumble and crack and refuse to form a pocket. Cut the pita into 2 even halves (to make 2 pockets), or slice about one-quarter off the top (to make 1 giant pocket). Carefully spread the sides apart, trying not to tear the bread.

Next, you have to leak-proof the pocket. Professionals recommend lining your pita with some sort of shredded green stuff. Lettuce or cabbage are very effective for this. Gently jam it down to the bottom of the pita.

Now plunk in whatever treasures you've found. Grated cheese, chopped tomato, cucumber, or onion, sliced meat or fish, canned beans, tuna, or salmon—anything at all. Experiment with weird and wonderful combinations of ingredients.

Drizzle a little salad dressing, mayonnaise (thinned with pickle juice), salsa, barbecue sauce—anything—into the top, sprinkle with salt and pepper, and eat.

OK, so it leaks a little. Catch the drips with a napkin.

Gazpacho

Look! In your bowl! Is it a soup? Is it a salad? Who cares? It's great.

3	cloves garlic, squished
4	ripe tomatoes
4 cups (1 L)	tomato or tomato-vegetable juice
1	small fresh hot pepper, seeds removed (very optional)
6	green onions, cut into chunks
2	stalks celery, cut into chunks
1	green pepper, cut into chunks
2	medium cucumbers, peeled and cut into chunks
¼ cup (50 mL)	lemon juice or vinegar
1 tsp (5 mL)	salt
½ tsp (2 mL)	pepper

In the container of a blender or food processor, combine the garlic, 2 of the tomatoes, and about half of the tomato juice and blend until puréed. Add the hot pepper, green onions, celery, green pepper, and cucumbers, and blend briefly, scraping the sides down a couple of times—this should stay a little chunky. Stir in the lemon juice or vinegar, the salt, pepper, and the rest of the tomato juice. Chop the remaining 2 tomatoes coarsely and stir them into the soup. Taste, and adjust seasoning with salt and pepper. Chill before serving, if possible. You can add a blob of sour cream or plain yogurt to each serving, if you want to really be élégant.

Makes about 6 servings.

Lumpy Mashed Potatoes

You'll definitely want this with your meat loaf.

6	medium potatoes, peeled and cubed
3 tbsp (50 mL)	butter
½ cup (125 mL)	hot milk
½ tsp (2 mL)	salt (or to taste)

First you'll need to cook the potatoes. If you have a steamer basket, place it into a medium saucepan, put some water in the bottom, add the potatoes to the basket, and steam until completely soft. (Poke a fork into a potato cube to make sure.) If you don't have a steamer basket, put the potatoes into the saucepan, add just enough water to cover them completely, bring to a boil, and cook until soft.

Drain the cooked potatoes thoroughly and mash them with a fork or a potato masher, if you have one. Try to get most (but not all) of the lumps out. Add the butter, hot milk, and salt and whip the potatoes with a fork until light and fluffy. Never use a mixer or a processor to mash potatoes because it will make the potatoes gluey, and you *definitely* don't want gluey.

Serve immediately, if possible, or cover the dish and keep warm in a warm oven (200° F) (100° C), until you want to serve them.

Makes about 4 normal servings, as a side dish.

Couch Potato Potatoes

There are times when a plate of crisp, hot fries are just the thing. These are delicious, addictive, and a zillion times better than frozen French fries.

5	medium potatoes, washed and cut into wedges (peel them if you want to)
¼ cup (50 mL)	vegetable oil
1 tbsp (15 mL)	lemon juice
	salt and pepper

Preheat the oven to 450° F (230° C).

Dump the potatoes into a 9 × 13-inch (22 × 33 cm) baking dish. Drizzle them with the vegetable oil, the lemon juice, sprinkle with salt and pepper, and toss to coat everything evenly. Spread the potato wedges out in the pan so that they're in one layer.

Bake at 450° F (230° C) for at least 45 minutes, stirring them around from time to time, until they're crisp and golden on the outside and nice and mushy on the inside.

Now, isn't that better than anything?

Scalloped Potatoes

Here's a side dish that really wants to be the main course. Go ahead, give it a chance.

6	medium potatoes, peeled and sliced very thin
2 tbsp (30 mL)	flour
1 tsp (5 mL)	salt
¼ tsp (1 mL)	pepper
1½ cups (375 mL)	grated cheddar or Swiss cheese (optional)
2 tbsp (30 mL)	butter or margarine
2½ cups (625 mL)	milk

Preheat the oven to 375° F (190° C).

Grease a 9 × 13-inch (22 × 33 cm) baking dish, and spread about ⅓ of the potato slices in the bottom, as evenly as possible. Sprinkle with about half each of the flour, salt, pepper, and cheese. Cover this with another ⅓ of the potato slices, then sprinkle with the rest of the flour, salt, pepper, and cheese. Finally, cover with the rest of the potato slices, dot the top with butter, and pour the milk over everything.

Cover the baking dish with foil, and bake at 375° F (190° C) for 30 minutes. Remove the foil and bake for another 30 to 40 minutes, until the potatoes feel done when you poke a knife into the middle, and the top is browned.

Makes 8 to 10 servings.

Refried Beans

Canned refried beans are salty, greasy, and really not that great. To make matters worse, some brands use lard, which you won't want to eat if you're a vegetarian. These beans take maybe twenty minutes to make, and are much (much) better.

½ cup (125 mL)	finely chopped onion
1	clove garlic, squished
2 tbsp (30 mL)	vegetable or olive oil
1 19-oz (540 mL)	can beans (red or white kidney, pinto, romano, or black) *or*
2½ cups (625 mL)	home-cooked beans (see directions on page 138)
	salt to taste

In a medium skillet, sauté the onion and the garlic in the oil for about 5 minutes over low heat, until soft. If you're using canned beans, add them, with all their liquid, to the pan. If you're using home-cooked beans, add the beans and about 1 cup (250 mL) of their cooking liquid to the pan. Cook, mashing with a wooden spoon or a potato masher, until the mixture is fairly thick and about half mashed. You can add a bit more liquid if you think they're too dry. Add salt to taste.

Use these beans to fill burritos (page 145), as a dip with tortilla chips and salsa, or in Fully Loaded Nachos (page 185).

Makes about 3 cups (750 mL) refried beans, to use in whatever way your little heart desires.

How to Cook Frozen Vegetables

A bag or two of frozen vegetables is a very good thing to keep around. They're cheap, don't go rotten, and taste fresher than canned. And, in deepest, darkest February, when even the crummiest cabbage costs a month's rent, you'll want to put something green on your plate, won't you?

Not all frozen veggies are created equal. Some frozen vegetables actually taste better than the "fresh" ones that have spent a couple of weeks hitchhiking from Mexico to get to your supermarket. Other frozen veggies might be worth buying because they're cheaper than fresh, a little more convenient, or available out of season.

The best of the frozen lot are peas, corn, green and yellow beans, broccoli, and cauliflower. Spinach is OK too, if the fresh stuff is looking a little shabby. And some of the vegetable mixtures are neat, if you just want a pile of different things to throw in a soup or stir-fry.

Frozen carrots are silly, since fresh ones are always good and much cheaper. Frozen asparagus and zucchini are disappointing, and frozen potatoes are just plain weird.

Whenever possible, buy the kind of frozen vegetables that are loose in bags. That way you can use just exactly what you need, reseal the bag, and toss it back into the freezer.

Regular cooking:
Bring a pot of water to a boil. Add the vegetables, let the water return to a boil, and cook for 2 to 8 minutes, depending on the vegetable and package instructions.

Steam cooking:
Place frozen vegetables in a steamer basket or colander over boiling water, and steam for 2 to 8 minutes, until they're done the way you like them.

Microwave cooking:
Put frozen vegetables in a microwave-safe dish, add 1 tbsp (15 mL) of water for each cup of vegetables and cover with a lid or plastic wrap. Microwave on high power for 3 to 5 minutes, stirring a couple of times.

How to Cook Rice

You don't need to ever use instant rice. Ever. The real thing tastes better, is cheaper, and doesn't take very much time to make anyway.

White Rice

Long-grain white rice is light, fluffy, and goes with anything.

2 cups (500 mL)   water
1 cup (250 mL)   long-grain white rice

Measure the water into a saucepan that has a tight-fitting lid. Bring it to a boil over high heat. Add the rice to the boiling water. Give it a stir, lower the heat to the barest simmer, and put the lid on the pot. Let it cook for 20 minutes without peeking.

After 20 minutes, lift the lid and have a look. The water should be completely absorbed, and the surface of the rice should look as if there are holes all over it. Don't stir, but taste a grain to see if it's cooked. If not, replace the lid and let it cook for another 5 minutes and taste again. Remove the pan from the heat, fluff with a fork, and serve.

Makes 3 cups (750 mL) of cooked white rice.

Brown Rice

Slightly chewy, nutty, delicious. Brown rice takes a little longer to cook, but it's terribly good for you, and it goes well with beans and other hearty things.

3 cups (750 mL)   water
1 cup (250 mL)   brown rice

Measure the water into a saucepan that has a tight-fitting lid. Bring it to a boil over high heat. Add the rice to the boiling water. Give it a stir, lower the heat to the barest simmer, and put the lid on the pot. Let it cook for 30 minutes without peeking.

After 30 minutes, lift the lid and have a look. The water should be completely absorbed, and the surface of the rice should look as if there are holes all over it. Don't stir, but taste a grain to see if it's cooked. If not, replace the lid and let it cook for another 5 minutes, then taste it again. Remove the pan from the heat, fluff with a fork, and serve.

Makes 4 cups (1000 mL) of cooked brown rice.

A Grainy Glossary

Long-grain white rice all-purpose rice that cooks up fluffy and white

Short-grain white rice stickier than long grain, and a little chewy; especially good for Chinese dishes

Basmati rice aromatic rice from India with a wonderfully nutty flavor

Arborio rice Italian short-grain rice, used in risotto and very good for rice pudding

Converted rice steamed before milling, this rice doesn't stick together when you cook it and has retained more of its vitamins than regular white rice

Instant rice this has been completely cooked, then dehydrated; useful for mountain climbing and other desperate survival situations

Brown rice this is what white rice was before they sanded the outsides off; very tasty, chewy, full of vitamins and other good stuff

Wild rice not really rice, but it looks sort of like it; very tasty, brown and chewy, and *very* expensive

Barley a delicious chewy grain, great in soup, and good as a side dish instead of rice

Millet this is actually birdseed—really; cheap, fast cooking, very delicious

Quinoa a rediscovered ancient Inca grain; extremely nutritious, high in protein and minerals

Couscous actually a very teensy little pasta, not an actual grain; made from wheat, it cooks in minutes

Bulgur wheat cracked wheat that has been completely cooked and then dehydrated—sort of like instant rice, only much tastier

Buckwheat (kasha) earthy-tasting grain, available either toasted or untoasted, it makes an excellent dish with mushrooms and onions

Mainly Meat
(Beef, Chicken, and Other Critters)

A Perfect Hamburger

Perfection, hamburgerwise, is in the eye of the beholder. Some people like theirs filled with stuff like chopped vegetables, bread crumbs, eggs, cheese. Others are purists and like their burgers straight. This is a compromise. A little bit of stuff, but not too much.

1 lb (500 g)	medium ground beef
2 tbsp (30 mL)	barbecue sauce, ketchup, mayonnaise, or salsa
2 tbsp (30 mL)	finely chopped onion (optional)
½ tsp (2 mL)	salt
¼ tsp (1 mL)	pepper

In a bowl, with a fork or barehanded, mix together the ground beef with the barbecue sauce (or whatever), the onion, the salt, and the pepper. Gently. The secret to a perfect burger is not to handle it too much, so don't mush it to death.

Handling the meat very lightly, form it into 3 or 4 patties, squishing them just enough so they don't fall apart. Flatten the burgers to an even thickness—about ½ inch (1 cm) is good. Your burgers will shrink as they cook.

Cook on the barbecue, under the broiler, or in a skillet, until no longer pink inside—turning over halfway through. Serve on a lightly toasted bun, with absolutely everything on it. Especially hot peppers.

Makes 3 large or 4 regular burgers. *Perfect* ones.

Plain Old Meatballs

These are meatballs searching for their identity. Should they settle for spaghetti? Or should they wait for something more exotic—and go Hawaiian? Or would they be wise to just go it alone on a toothpick? Only you can help.

1 lb (500 g)	medium ground beef (or turkey)
1	egg
½ cup (125 mL)	bread crumbs
¼ cup (50 mL)	*very* finely chopped onion
1 tsp (5 mL)	salt
½ tsp (2 mL)	pepper

In a medium bowl, combine the ground beef, egg, bread crumbs, onion, salt, and pepper. Squish together with a fork or clean bare hands until well mixed. Form into 1-inch (2 cm) meatballs, rolling them between your hands so they're nice and round. Place meatballs in one layer on a cookie sheet and bake at 375° F (190° C) for 15 to 20 minutes, turning them over halfway through baking.

Scoop the meatballs off the cookie sheet, leaving behind the fat that has drained out of them, and use in any recipe that calls for Plain Old Meatballs, such as Hawaiian Meatballs (page 71), Killer Barbecue Meatballs (page 72), or Spaghetti with Meatballs (page 108).

Hawaiian Meatballs

*If it has pineapple in it, it must be from Hawaii, right? Well, maybe.
Anyway, it's good.*

1 14-oz (398 mL)	**can pineapple chunks**
¼ cup (50 mL)	**brown sugar**
2 tbsp (30 mL)	**cornstarch**
½ tsp (2 mL)	**ground ginger**
1 tbsp (15 mL)	**soy sauce**
3 tbsp (45 mL)	**vinegar**
1 batch	**Plain Old Meatballs (recipe on page 70)**
1	**green pepper, cut into large squares**
1	**onion, cut into large squares**

Drain the pineapple chunks, pouring the juice into a measuring cup.
Add enough water to the juice to make 1¼ cups (300 mL) of liquid.
Pour this into a saucepan. (Try to restrain yourself from eating all the
pineapple chunks—you'll be needing them later.) Add to the juice in
the saucepan the brown sugar, cornstarch, ginger, soy sauce, and vinegar.
Bring to a simmer over medium heat, stirring constantly, until the
sauce is clear and thickened. Dump in the entire batch of Plain Old
Meatballs, cooked and drained, and let them simmer in the sauce for
5 minutes. Add the green pepper, the onion, and the pineapple chunks,
bring to a boil, and cook for about 5 minutes more. Serve over rice.

Makes about 4 servings.

Killer Barbecue Meatballs

Are you daring enough to face these extra-spicy meatballs?

¼ cup (50 mL)	vegetable oil
2	onions, chopped
4	cloves garlic, squished
1 28-oz (796 mL)	can tomatoes, drained and mashed
1 5½-oz (156 mL)	can tomato paste
1 tsp (5 mL)	hot pepper sauce (or more, or less)
2 tbsp (30 mL)	dry mustard
2 tbsp (30 mL)	sugar
1 tbsp (15 mL)	vinegar
1 tsp (5 mL)	salt
½ tsp (2 mL)	pepper
1 batch	Plain Old Meatballs (page 70)

Heat the oil in a large skillet. Add the onions and garlic and sauté over medium heat for about 5 minutes, until soft. Add all the remaining ingredients except the meatballs, bring to a boil, and simmer for 10 to 15 minutes, stirring once in a while. Sauce should be slightly thickened.

Plunk the browned meatballs into the simmering sauce, and continue to cook, stirring, for another 15 to 20 minutes.

Serve meatballs over rice, or with potatoes, or as a munchie with toothpicks.

Makes about 4 servings, as a meal.

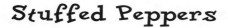

Stuffed Peppers

Stuffing a pepper is a very satisfying thing to do. They don't require any fancy folding, they're sturdy enough to withstand a certain amount of abuse, and they bounce rather nicely if you happen to drop one on the floor (not on purpose).

1 lb (500 g)	lean ground beef or turkey
½ cup (125 mL)	raw white rice
1	small onion, chopped
1	egg
	salt and pepper to taste
6 to 8	small green (or red) peppers
3 tbsp (45 mL)	vegetable oil
2 tbsp (30 mL)	flour
1 48-oz (1.36 L)	can tomato juice

In a medium bowl, combine the beef (or turkey), rice, onion, egg, and seasonings. Stir with a fork or mush with your (clean) bare hands until well mixed.

Prepare the green peppers by cutting around the stem end of each pepper and removing the stem and seed clump. Rinse out the cavity.

Stuff the peppers with the meat mixture, filling them just to about ½ inch (1 cm) from the top (the stuffing will expand as it cooks). This amount of stuffing should fill 6 to 8 peppers. If you run out of peppers before you run out of stuffing, just form the meat into little balls and toss them into the sauce to cook.

In a very large pot, combine the vegetable oil with the flour, and cook gently over low heat for 1 or 2 minutes, stirring constantly. Pour the tomato juice in gradually, and bring to a boil, stirring to avoid lumps. The sauce will thicken slightly.

Carefully lower the stuffed peppers into the boiling tomato sauce, making sure the sauce just covers the tops of the peppers. If it doesn't, add a little water to bring up the level of the liquid. Cover, and simmer the peppers gently over low heat for 1½ hours, stirring gently from time to time to keep the bottom from sticking.

Serve stuffed peppers nicely drowned in the tomato sauce.

Makes 4 to 6 servings.

*Surprise bonus: The leftover sauce (there is always some sauce left over) makes a great tomato soup with a couple of crackers crumbled into it.

Six-Layer Casserole

This is a complete no-brainer. And a microwave one, at that.

2	medium potatoes, sliced
2	medium onions, peeled and sliced
1½ lbs (750 g)	lean ground beef or turkey
½ cup (125 mL)	raw rice
2	stalks celery, sliced
3	medium carrots, peeled and sliced
2 cups (500 mL)	chicken broth (diluted canned, or made from a cube or powder)

Before you do anything else, assemble all the ingredients. Slice up the potatoes, onions, celery, and carrots; measure the rice and the broth.

Using a large, round, microwave-safe casserole, evenly layer the ingredients in the following order: potatoes on the bottom, then the onions, the ground beef, the rice, the celery, and the carrots. Sprinkle each layer as you go with a little salt and pepper. Finally, pour the broth over the whole business and cover the casserole with a lid (if it has one). If it doesn't, cover it with plastic wrap and cut a little vent hole into the top so that it doesn't blow up.

Microwave on high power for 15 minutes. Give the casserole a quarter turn (it will cook more evenly), then microwave on medium power for 45 minutes longer, turning the dish every 15 minutes or so, if you think of it.

Let the dish stand, covered, for about 10 minutes after taking it out of the oven, to allow it to finish cooking.

Makes about 6 servings.

The Ultimate Sloppy Joe

Most Sloppy Joes look as if they started out as something else that never quite got finished. But not these. Go no further—you've arrived at Sloppy Joe perfection.

3 tbsp (45 mL)	vegetable oil
1	onion, chopped
1	stalk celery, chopped
1 cup (250 mL)	chopped mushrooms
1 lb (500 g)	medium ground beef or ground turkey
¼ cup (50 mL)	beef broth
¼ cup (50 mL)	ketchup
½ tsp (2 mL)	hot pepper sauce (or more, or less, or none)

Heat the oil in a large skillet, add the onion, celery, and mushrooms and cook over medium heat until soft, 7 to 10 minutes. Add the ground beef or turkey and cook, stirring to break up the lumps, until the meat is no longer pink, about 5 to 7 minutes. Add the beef broth, the ketchup, and the hot pepper sauce, and simmer for another 5 minutes, until everything is nicely glopped together.

Spoon over 4 toasted hamburger buns and eat, sloppily.

Curly Noodle Dinner

Absolutely idiotically easy, this is the fastest emergency dinner there is—fifteen minutes from start to finish.

1 lb (500 g)	medium ground beef
1	package oriental noodle soup, any flavor
1 12-oz (341 mL)	can corn niblets, drained
1 19-oz (540 mL)	can *stewed* tomatoes—plain or a snazzy seasoned kind

In a large skillet, cook the ground beef until browned. Drain off the fat (not down the sink, please).

Add the flavor packet from the noodles, the corn, and the stewed tomatoes. Bring to a boil. Crumble in the noodles and cook, covered, for about 10 minutes. That's it.

Serves 3 or 4.

Totally Excellent Chili

To be totally excellent, a chili must be spicy (but not necessarily hot), and runny enough to eat with a spoon, but not soupy. Leave out the hot pepper or cayenne if you prefer a mild chili—it will still have plenty of kick.

1½ lb (750 g)	lean ground beef
2	large onions, chopped
2	cloves garlic, squished
1 28-oz (796 mL)	can tomatoes
2 tsp (10 mL)	chili powder
½ tsp (2 mL)	curry powder
2 tsp (10 mL)	ground cumin
1	small fresh hot pepper, chopped *or*
¼ tsp (1 mL)	cayenne pepper
2 tsp (10 mL)	salt
2 19-oz (540 mL)	cans red kidney beans, drained and rinsed

In a large skillet, cook the beef, stirring to break up clumps, with the onions and garlic until the meat is no longer pink. Add the canned tomatoes (with all their juice) and the seasonings, and simmer for about 30 minutes, mashing the tomatoes with a wooden spoon to break them up. Add the beans and cook for another 30 minutes.

Serve this Totally Excellent Chili over plain rice, sprinkled with shredded cheese.

Makes about 6 servings.

Red Beans and Rice

Beans and rice go together like, um, shoes and socks. Only they taste much better. Vegetarians can omit the bacon and use vegetable broth or tomato juice instead of the beef broth in this recipe.

6 slices	bacon, cut into 1-inch (2 cm) pieces
2	onions, cut into ½-inch (1 cm) wedges
1	garlic clove, squished
2½ cups (625 mL)	beef broth (reconstituted canned, or from bouillon powder or cubes)
1 cup (250 mL)	white rice
½ cup (125 mL)	diced green pepper
1 tsp (5 mL)	thyme
2 19-oz (540 mL)	cans red kidney beans, drained and rinsed
1 tbsp (15 mL)	chopped fresh parsley (optional)

Cook the bacon in a medium skillet until browned, but not really totally crisp, about 5 minutes. Remove the bacon pieces from the skillet, and drain off all but about a tablespoon of the fat (*not down the sink!*— you can pour it into a tin can or a cup and scoop it out and into the garbage when it cools and solidifies). Add the onion and garlic to the skillet and cook for about 5 minutes, until softened.

Pour the beef broth into the pan and bring it to a boil, stirring to dissolve the brown bits on the bottom of the pan. Add the rice, the bacon pieces, the green pepper, and the thyme. Cover tightly, lower the heat, and simmer for 15 minutes. Stir in the beans, and cook for another 5 minutes. Sprinkle with chopped parsley (if you're using it) before serving.

Makes 4 servings.

Twenty-Minute Tacos

It's midnight. You need tacos. Can you wait twenty minutes?

1 lb (500 g)	ground beef (or chicken, or turkey)
½ cup (125 mL)	chopped onion
½ cup (125 mL)	chopped green pepper
1	clove garlic, squished
1 cup (250 mL)	tomato sauce (any kind—even leftover spaghetti sauce is fine)
1 tsp (5 mL)	Worcestershire sauce
¼ tsp (1 mL)	cayenne pepper (or more, or less)
1 tsp (5 mL)	chili powder
½ tsp (2 mL)	salt
12-ish	taco shells or flour tortillas (if you like soft tacos)
	taco stuff: shredded lettuce, diced tomatoes, salsa, shredded cheese, sour cream, chopped onions, diced avocado, jalapeño peppers, chocolate chips (just kidding)

In a large skillet, combine the ground beef (or whatever), the onion, green pepper, and garlic. Cook over medium heat, stirring to break up lumps, for 8 to 10 minutes, until the meat is browned and the onions and green pepper are softened. Drain as much of the fat out of the pan as possible—either by pouring into an empty can (not down the sink), or by scooping it out with a large spoon.

Add the tomato sauce, Worcestershire sauce, cayenne, chili powder, and salt. Cook, stirring, over medium heat for 7 to 10 minutes, until the mixture is thick enough to spoon into a taco shell without running out the sides.

Heat taco shells at 300° F (160° C) for 10 minutes (or warm foil-wrapped tortillas the same way), then fill them with the meat mixture. Top with some taco stuff and eat. Quick! Make another!

Makes about 12 tacos.

Mom's Dreaded Meat Loaf

Did your Mom make this every Wednesday? Did you have to take meatloaf sandwiches to school? Did you hate them? Do you miss it now? Here—make this.

1½ lbs (750 g)	medium ground beef
1 cup (250 mL)	soft white bread crumbs
2	eggs, beaten
1	small onion, finely chopped
2 tsp (10 mL)	beef bouillon powder (or 2 cubes)
¼ tsp (1 mL)	pepper (or to taste)
1 cup (250 mL)	tomato juice
¼ cup (50 mL)	ketchup
1 or 2	hard-boiled eggs, peeled (optional)

Combine all the ingredients, except the ketchup and the hard-boiled eggs, in a large bowl, using your bare hands or a large fork to mix. (Barehanded meatloaf mixing is a truly primal experience, and highly recommended.) Don't forget to wash your hands before and afterward.

Now, at this point, you have 2 choices: You can either squish the mixture into a loaf pan to bake (simple, straightforward, very fast); or you can make a free form loaf by hand and bake it in a shallow pan (this allows for more creative expression). Clearly, you'll want to make your meat loaf exactly the way your mom made it.

What to do with the hard-boiled eggs? So glad you asked. Bury them in the center of the loaf as a sort of hidden treasure. Looks nice sliced, but not critical to the success of the actual loaf.

Paint the surface of the meat loaf with the ketchup, and bake at 350° F (180° C) for 1 hour and 15 minutes. Let stand 5 to 10 minutes before slicing.

Eat with mashed potatoes and something green.

Makes 5 to 6 servings.

Shepherd's Pie

You don't have to be a shepherd to make this dish. Or to love it.

2 tbsp (30 mL)	vegetable oil
1	onion, chopped
2	cloves garlic, squished
1	green or red pepper, diced
1	carrot, diced
2 cups (500 mL)	sliced fresh mushrooms
1½ lbs (750 g)	*lean* ground beef or ground turkey
1 cup (250 mL)	frozen peas
1 cup (250 mL)	ketchup *or* salsa *or* chili sauce
4	large potatoes, peeled and cut into chunks
2 tbsp (30 mL)	butter
½ cup (125 mL)	milk
	salt and pepper to taste, and a little paprika

Heat the vegetable oil in a large skillet. Add the onion and garlic, and cook for a couple of minutes, until softened. Add the peppers, carrots, and mushrooms, and cook for 5 to 7 minutes, until the carrots are almost tender.

Add the ground beef or turkey to the skillet and cook, stirring to break up the clumps for about 10 minutes, until the meat is lightly browned. Add the peas, stir in the ketchup (or whatever), and cook for another 10 minutes. Season with salt and pepper, and dump into an 8- or 9-inch (20 or 22 cm) square baking dish.

While the meat mixture is cooking, make the mashed potatoes. Cook the potatoes in boiling water (or steam them in a steamer) until completely tender when poked with a fork, then drain thoroughly. Return them to the pot in which they were cooked, and mash them as smooth as you possibly can, adding the butter, milk, and a little salt and pepper. Spread the mashed potatoes, while they are still warm, over the meat mixture in the baking dish. A sprinkle of paprika on top is a cheery touch.

Bake at 350° F (180° C) for 35 to 40 minutes, until the top is golden and the meat is bubbling underneath.

Makes 4 to 6 servings.

Basic Beef Stew

Sometimes a good old bowl of stew is just the thing. Serve it with
some decent bread and a salad, and you'll feel very happy.

1 tbsp (15 mL)	flour
½ tsp (2 mL)	salt
¼ tsp (1 mL)	pepper
2 lbs (1 kg)	beef stewing meat, cut into 1-inch (2 cm) cubes
1 tbsp (15 mL)	vegetable oil
2½ cups (625 mL)	tomato juice
1	onion, chopped
1 tsp (5 mL)	crumbled basil or oregano
2	medium potatoes, peeled and cubed
2	medium carrots, cut into 1-inch (2 cm) pieces
¼ cup (50 mL)	water (or red wine, if you happen to have some around)

Preheat the oven to 375° F (190° C).

Combine the flour with the salt and pepper in a small bowl, and toss the cubes of meat in this mixture until they are coated. Heat the vegetable oil in a pot with a tight-fitting lid that can go into the oven (a Dutch oven is good), add the beef cubes, and cook them over medium heat, turning to brown all sides of the meat. Add the tomato juice, the chopped onion, and the basil or oregano, and stir. Cover pot and bake at 375° F (190° C) for 1 hour. Now add the potatoes, the carrots, and the water (or wine). Replace the cover, and continue baking for at least 1 more hour. The meat should be tender when you stick a fork in it. If it isn't, then let it bake another half hour or so, and test again.

Makes 3 to 4 servings.

Good Old Pot Roast

Make pot roast when you expect to be hanging around the house all day. It takes a long time to transform a tough hunk of meat into such a delicious dinner.

2 tbsp (30 mL)	vegetable oil
3 to 4 lb (1½ to 2 kg)	beef pot roast (see page 28 for suitable cuts), boneless or not
¼ cup (50 mL)	vinegar (cider or wine vinegar is best, but white will do)
¼ cup (50 mL)	ketchup
2 tbsp (30 mL)	soy sauce
2 tbsp (30 mL)	Worcestershire sauce
1 tsp (5 mL)	crumbled rosemary *or* thyme *or* oregano (or a little of each)
2	cloves garlic, squished
2 tsp (10 mL)	mustard
3	medium potatoes, cut into large chunks
3	medium carrots, cut into 1-inch (3 cm) pieces
1½ cups (375 mL)	small whole onions, peeled (or 2 to 3 medium ones, cut into quarters)

In a large pot with a lid (a Dutch oven is good), heat the vegetable oil over medium heat. Add the roast to the pot, turning it over and over until all the sides of the hunk are browned and crusty. Sprinkle the meat with salt and pepper.

In a bowl, combine the vinegar, ketchup, soy sauce, Worcestershire sauce, herbs, garlic, and mustard. Pour this mixture over the meat, cover it tightly with the lid, and let it simmer over low heat for 1½ hours.

Add the potatoes, carrots, and onions to the pot, arranging them around the meat so that everything fits. Put the cover back on and simmer for 1 more hour.

To serve, remove the meat from the pot, slice it thickly (it may fall apart, which is very comforting), and arrange it on a platter. Surround with the vegetables that have been fished out of the pot. Pour the pan juices into a small dish or pitcher, and serve with the meat and vegetables.

Makes 6 to 8 servings.

Forgotten Lamb Stew

Layer all the ingredients in a large, heavy stewpot, set it on the stove and, basically, forget about it. But not completely. Don't leave town or anything. Dinner will be ready in a couple of hours (or so).

2 lbs (1 kg)	boneless lamb shoulder, cut into 1-inch (2 cm) cubes
4	medium potatoes, sliced ½ inch (1 cm) thick
1	large onion, sliced
2	stalks celery, sliced
4	medium carrots, peeled and sliced
1 tsp (5 mL)	salt
	pepper to taste
½ tsp (2 mL)	thyme
1 cup (250 mL)	water
2 tbsp (30 mL)	flour
½ cup (125 mL)	cold water
2 tbsp (30 mL)	chopped fresh dill or parsley

Cut up all the ingredients, then layer them in a large pot (with a tight-fitting lid) in the following order: first the lamb cubes, then the potatoes, the onion, the celery, and finally the carrots. Sprinkle each layer with a little salt, pepper, and thyme.

Pour the cup (250 mL) of water into the pot, cover it, and bring it very slowly to a boil over medium-low heat. Lower the heat so that the mixture is just *barely simmering*, then go away and do your homework or something for about 2½ hours. Don't stir this while it's cooking. Really.

In a small bowl, whisk the flour into the ½ cup (125 mL) of cold water to make a smooth mixture. Remove the lid of the pot, pour in the flour mixture and very gently stir the forgotten stew (try not to smash up the potatoes), cooking until the liquid has thickened. Add the dill or parsley and cook for another minute or two.

Serves 4.

Unfried Chicken (or Fish)

Better than take-out, crisp, delicious, easy. Why would anyone not make this?

1 cup (250 mL)	**bread crumbs**
1 tbsp (15 mL)	**grated Parmesan cheese**
1 tsp (5 mL)	**oregano or Italian seasoning**
½ tsp (2 mL)	**salt**
¼ tsp (1 mL)	**pepper**
2-3 tbsp (30-45 mL)	**vegetable oil**
2½-3½ lbs (1-1.5 kg)	**chicken pieces, or one medium chicken, cut up**

Preheat the oven to 375° F (190° C).

In a plastic or paper bag combine the bread crumbs, Parmesan cheese, oregano (or whatever), salt, and pepper. Hold the top of the bag shut and shake to mix everything together.

Pour the vegetable oil into a small bowl and, using a pastry brush (or a *clean* paintbrush), brush the chicken pieces with the oil. Put 2 or 3 pieces of chicken at a time into the bag, and shake them until they are well coated with crumbs. Take them out of the bag and put the pieces on a rack that has been placed on a baking sheet. (The rack allows the fat to drain away from the chicken.)

Bake at 375° F (190° C) for 25 minutes, turn the pieces over, and bake for another 20 to 25 minutes, until golden brown. You can be sure the chicken is done if the juice runs clear (not pink) when you poke a fork into it.

Makes 3 or 4 servings.

Fish option: Use 1 lb (500 g) fish fillets instead of the chicken pieces in the above recipe. Bake for 10 to 20 minutes, until the fish flakes when you try to pry it apart with a fork.

How to Cut Up a Chicken

Oh, yuck. You've got yourself a whole chicken, and now you have to dismantle it. And though you don't need a degree in veterinary medicine to take a chicken apart, it might be helpful to get to know your victim before you begin.

Lay the bird out on the counter, belly up, and examine it for a couple of minutes. Move the various appendages so that you can feel where the joints are, and how it all hooks together. Flap the wings, walk it around on its drumsticks, have it do a little chicken dance around the room. Sound effects are helpful here, just to get into the mood. OK, that's enough. Now get to work.

Using a sharp knife or, better yet, a pair of good, sharp kitchen shears, cut the chicken lengthwise through the breast from the tail end to the neck end. Now, open the chicken up like a book, and cut alongside the backbone from one end to the other. Now you have 2 more or less identical halves. Feeling for the joint where it attaches to the body, cut the drumstick off. There is a place where it detaches fairly easily, so keep poking around with your knife until you find the right spot. Next, remove the wing in a similar fashion. Finally, separate the breast from the thigh by cutting the 2 sections apart along the curve of the thigh section, and with an extra little whack, cut the backbone in half. There. Now do the same thing to the other half.

If you have followed these instructions, you will end up with 2 drumsticks, 2 wings, 2 breasts, and 2 thighs. If you have gone berserk, you may have more pieces. You can now either cook the entire bird, or cook some of it, and wrap the remaining pieces individually in foil or plastic freezer bags to freeze them for a rainy day. Don't forget to label the packages!

Incredible Garlic Chicken

This recipe is not a joke. Not only is it totally delicious and very easy to make, but it is also absolutely guaranteed to protect you against vampires. An old Transylvanian recipe. Just kidding.

1 4-lb (2 kg)	**chicken**
	salt, pepper, thyme, rosemary, bay leaves, whatever
2 tbsp (30 mL)	**olive oil**
⅔ cup (150 mL)	**white wine (or chicken broth)**
40	**cloves of garlic—separate them, but leave the skins on (really)**

Preheat the oven to 375° F (190° C).

Wash the chicken, then pat it dry with paper towel. With your bare hands, rub the chicken inside and out with plenty of salt and pepper. (Then wash your hands.)

In a large skillet, heat the olive oil and brown the whole chicken in it, turning it over to do all the sides. Remove chicken from the pan and place it in a large casserole or (ovenproof) Dutch oven.

Pour the wine or broth into the skillet, stirring around to loosen the browned bits from the bottom of the pan (this is called "deglazing," by the way). Add this liquid to the casserole with the chicken.

Sprinkle in some thyme, a little rosemary, and a couple of bay leaves. Finally, toss in the garlic cloves. I'm not kidding about the number— *40 cloves*—and *don't* peel them. Trust me.

Cover the casserole tightly with a lid (or use foil if you don't have a lid to fit), and bake at 375° F (190° C) for 1¼ to 1½ hours. And don't peek while it's cooking.

Serve the cooked garlic cloves along with the chicken—they turn squishy and delicious, and are unbelievably amazing spread on some French or Italian bread (or just sucked out of their skins).

Serves 3 or 4.

Eat a few handfuls of parsley before going out in public.

Good Old Roast Chicken

Almost everyone likes roast chicken. It's familiar, delicious, and very homey. Plus, it makes for great leftovers the next day—if there are any leftovers, that is.

3 to 4 lb (1.5 to 2 kg)	whole chicken
2	cloves garlic, squished
1 tsp (5 mL)	salt
½ tsp (2 mL)	pepper
1 tsp (5 mL)	paprika
1 tbsp (15 mL)	vegetable oil

Preheat the oven to 375° F (190° C).

Wash the chicken under cold running water, inside and out, and dry it with paper towels. In a little bowl, combine the garlic, salt, pepper, paprika, and vegetable oil, stirring to make a fairly thick paste.

By hand, or with a basting brush (if you have such a thing), rub the garlic paste all over the chicken, inside and outside. (Pretend you're doing sunscreen at the beach.) Now, at this point, *some* people would truss the bird up with string—tying the legs together and the wings in tight to the body. The idea is to make the bird into a nice tight package so that there are no outlying appendages to overcook, but it isn't absolutely essential. You *can* get away without trussing.

Put the chicken into a roasting pan—an oblong baking pan or even a disposable foil pan—and roast at 375° F (190° C) for 1½ to 2 hours, basting with the pan juices once in a while, until the chicken is a deep golden brown and the leg moves easily when you jiggle it. If you're not absolutely sure that it's cooked, stab the chicken with a fork—the juices should be clear, not pink. Remove from the oven and let it cool for about 5 minutes before you try to cut it up—it will be easier to handle and won't leak quite as much.

Serves, oh, maybe 3 or 4, depending on whom you're feeding and exactly how big the chicken is.

Not Your Mom's Chicken and Dumplings

If your mom made chicken and dumplings, this is probably not it. But it's good, it has chicken in it, and (most important) it has dumplings. What more do you want?

4	boneless, skinless chicken breasts
6	potatoes
4	carrots
3	stalks celery
2	onions
4 cups (1 L)	chicken broth (homemade or canned)
1 tbsp (15 mL)	chopped fresh parsley
	salt and pepper to taste
1 cup (250 mL)	frozen peas
¾ cup (175 mL)	flour
¼ cup (50 mL)	cornmeal
2 tsp (10 mL)	baking powder
¼ tsp (1 mL)	salt
½ cup (125 mL)	milk
2 tbsp (30 mL)	vegetable oil

Cut the chicken, potatoes, carrots, and celery into approximately 1-inch (2 cm) chunks. Chop the onion into slightly smaller dice. Combine everything in a large saucepan or Dutch oven, then add the chicken broth, the chopped parsley, and the salt and pepper. If you are using canned broth, don't add any additional salt—you won't need it. Bring to a boil over high heat, then reduce the heat and simmer, covered, for 20 minutes. Stir in the peas.

Meanwhile, in a bowl, mix together the flour, cornmeal, baking powder, and salt. Stir in the milk and oil, and mix just until thoroughly moistened. Drop the dumpling batter by spoonfuls into the simmering stew (there should be 7 or 8 clumps). Cook, covered, for 15 minutes. Don't lift the lid, don't peek, don't do anything. It will be fine, I promise.

Makes 4 very comforting servings.

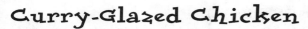

Curry-Glazed Chicken

What a dilemma. You want to appear sophisticated, worldly, slightly daring. But at the same time, you don't want to go too far because maybe your dinner guest isn't particularly daring or worldly. You'll need to compromise. Try this.

1 tbsp (15 mL)	butter
¼ cup (50 mL)	honey
3 tbsp (45 mL)	Dijon mustard
2 tsp (10 mL)	curry powder
½ tsp (2 mL)	salt
1 3-lb (1.5 kg)	chicken, cut up into serving pieces

Preheat the oven to 375° F (190° C). While the oven is preheating, measure the butter into a 9 × 13-inch (22 × 33 cm) baking dish, and put it into the oven to melt.

When the butter is melted, remove the pan from the oven and stir in the honey, the mustard, the curry powder, and the salt. Add the chicken pieces to the pan, turning them over to coat with the honey mixture on all sides.

Bake at 375° F (190° C) for 45 minutes, turning the chicken pieces over after 20 minutes.

Serve with something that will sop up the delicious sauce—like rice or couscous.

Makes 3 or 4 servings.

Honey Garlic Wings

If you eat this with your hands, sitting in front of the TV, then it's a snack. On a plate, at the table, it's a meal. Either way, these wings are delicious.

3 lbs (1.5 kg)	chicken wings
1 tsp (5 mL)	ground ginger
3	cloves garlic
1 cup (250 mL)	honey or brown sugar
¼ cup (50 mL)	soy sauce
1 tbsp (15 mL)	vinegar
½ cup (125 mL)	water

Preheat the oven to 375° F (190° C).

Trim the pointy tips off each wing and discard them (or save to add to chicken soup). Cut each wing in half at the elbow. Arrange them in one layer in a baking dish, just large enough to hold them all.

In a food processor or blender, combine the ginger, garlic, honey or sugar, soy sauce, vinegar, and water. Whirl until smooth. Pour this mixture over the wings, and toss them around a bit until they're all coated. Bake at 375° F (190° C) for 15 minutes, turn them over in the sauce, and bake for another 15 to 20 minutes, until the wings are browned and the sauce is nice and sticky.

Eat them just like that, straight from the pan, or be grown up about it and serve it with some rice to sop up the extra sauce.

Makes 3 to 4 servings.

Thermonuclear Chicken Wings

Traditionally served with celery sticks (just plain celery sticks) and blue cheese dressing (ditto), these wings are an easy version of the Buffalo classic. To avoid Total Meltdown, you may, if absolutely necessary, reduce the amount of hot pepper sauce.

12	chicken wings (about 2 lbs/1 kg)
½ cup (125 mL)	flour
¼ cup (50 mL)	butter
3 tbsp (45 mL)	hot pepper sauce (or *less* for the timid, or *more* for the brave)
1 tbsp (15 mL)	vinegar

Preheat the oven to 375° F (190° C).

Trim the pointy tips off each wing and discard them (or save to add to chicken soup). Cut each wing in half at the elbow. Put the flour into a small bag, toss in 3 or 4 pieces of wing at a time, hold the top closed and shake until coated. Remove the wings to a baking sheet and repeat until all the wings are floured. Bake at 375° F (190° C) for 15 minutes, then turn the wings over, and bake another 15 minutes, or until crisp.

While the wings are baking, melt the butter with the hot pepper sauce and the vinegar in a small saucepan. Stir to mix, and remove from heat. As soon as the wings are done, remove them to a bowl and toss with the hot sauce mixture. Serve immediately, if you dare.

Makes 2 to 4 servings, but this is being optimistic.

Cooking a Whole Turkey

Cooking a whole turkey isn't a crazy thing to do. Turkey is cheap, delicious, and easy to cook. Leftover turkey makes the world's best sandwich (with plenty of mayo), and the bones are great for soup. If you're afraid of tackling an entire turkey, practice on a chicken first (see recipe on page 87). It's the same thing, only smaller.

If your turkey is frozen, let it thaw *in the refrigerator*. Depending on the size of the bird, this could take anywhere from overnight to a couple of days. Leaving a frozen turkey out to thaw at room temperature is an excellent way to breed the sorts of bacteria you might have studied in science class but you certainly don't want to eat. An *unfrozen* turkey will just need to be washed and patted dry before you proceed. In either case, make sure you check inside the cavity for that cute little surprise packet (liver, heart, other innards), which must be removed. You can use it to make soup, cook and feed to the cat, or pull a juvenile practical joke on a friend.

1	**turkey, any size, washed and patted dry**
2 tbsp (30 mL)	**vegetable oil**
2 tsp (10 mL)	**salt**
1 tsp (5 mL)	**pepper**
2 tsp (10 mL)	**paprika**
4	**cloves garlic, squished**

Preheat the oven to 325° F (160° C).

In a small bowl, mash together the vegetable oil, salt, pepper, paprika, and garlic. By hand (but wash your hands before you touch other food) or with a brush (if you're the squeamish type) apply this mixture to the turkey, inside and out, the way you'd smear sunscreen on at the beach. Stuff the turkey, if you want (see recipe, page 93), or leave it unstuffed.

Tie the turkey's legs together with some string, and tie the wings in close to the body. The idea is to make as compact a package as possible so that there are no sticking-out parts to overcook before the rest of the turkey is done.

Put the turkey into an uncovered roasting pan and put it in the pre-heated oven. For the first hour, baste the turkey often (like, every

10 minutes or so) with some melted butter or vegetable oil. Once the juices start to collect in the bottom of the pan, use those to baste the bird—and keep basting every 20 minutes, or whenever you think of it. Basting helps to keep the bird moist and gives it that nice crunchy skin everyone loves. Cooking time will depend on the size of your turkey:

Roasting times at 325° F (160° C):

Weight		Roasting time	
lbs	kgs	stuffed	unstuffed
6–8	3–3.5	3–3¼ hrs.	2½–2¾ hrs.
8–10	3.5–4.5	3¼–3½ hrs.	2¾–3 hrs.
10–12	4.5–5.5	3½–3¾ hrs.	3–3¼ hrs.
12–16	5.5–7	3¾–4 hrs.	3¼–3½ hrs.
16–22	7–10	4–4½ hrs.	3½–4 hrs.

When the turkey's done, its leg will wiggle easily, the juices will run clear when you poke it with a knife, and if you happen to have a meat thermometer (!) it will register 170° F (77° C) for an unstuffed turkey, or 180° F (82° C) for a stuffed one. Remove from the oven, and let the bird rest (it's had a hard day) for 15 to 20 minutes before scooping the stuffing out, and cutting the turkey up.

Spoon the pan juices into a bowl, and serve it with the turkey just the way it is. Of course, if you want to go to the trouble of making gravy (recipe on page 93), go right ahead. But this is pretty good too. If anyone complains, just say it's the way they serve it France. Or something.

Oh, and don't forget the cranberry sauce.

Important safety bulletin!!! *Never leave stuffing inside a turkey for any length of time either before or after it has been cooked. The interior of a turkey is an amazing breeding ground for the kind of bacteria you don't want to feed to anyone you like. Stuff a turkey just before cooking it, and remove the stuffing immediately after it's done. This is not a joke.*

Stuffing—the best part of the turkey

The next time you're at a turkey dinner watch to see what people eat first. Hint: it's not the brussels sprouts.

¼ cup (50 mL)	vegetable oil
1	onion, chopped
1	stalk celery, finely chopped
8 cups (2 L)	slightly stale bread, crumbled by hand into small shreds
¼ cup (50 mL)	finely chopped fresh parsley
¼ tsp (1 mL)	salt
¼ tsp (1 mL)	pepper
1 tbsp (15 mL)	sage or poultry seasoning

Heat the oil in a small skillet, add the onion and celery and sauté for 5 to 8 minutes, until softened.

In a large bowl, combine the crumbled bread, the parsley, salt, pepper, and seasoning. Add the onion mixture, and toss to combine. Taste to see if it needs any more salt or pepper, then use to stuff the turkey before tying it up.

This makes enough stuffing for an 8 to 10 lb (4 to 5 kg) turkey. And there's no law that says you can't use it for a chicken.

Gravy—the second best part of the turkey

While your turkey is, um, resting, make this gravy.

¼ cup (50 mL)	fat from the roasting pan
2 cups (500 mL)	turkey broth, water, or a combination
¼ cup (50 mL)	flour

After your turkey is finished roasting, remove it from the pan and drain all the pan juices into a bowl, leaving them to settle for a few minutes. Meanwhile, pour the 2 cups (500 mL) of water or broth into the (now empty) roasting pan, and swish them around, scraping the bottom with a wooden spoon, to dissolve the delicious crusty stuff on the pan.

Measure ¼ cup (50 mL) of the fat that is floating on top of the pan juices and pour it into a saucepan. Skim all the rest of the fat off, and discard it—but hang on to the juices. Add the flour to the fat in the saucepan, stir to blend, and cook for 1 or 2 minutes. Stir in the reserved juices and the liquid that was swishing around the roasting pan. Cook over low heat, stirring constantly, until thickened—at least 5 minutes.

Makes about 3 cups (750 mL) of the best gravy you'll ever taste.

The Leftover Zone

Leftovers are your friends. They are always there for you, waiting patiently in the fridge, ready to be eaten at any moment. Why do we treat them so badly? Here are some ways to show those loyal leftovers how much we really appreciate them.

Heat them up and serve just the way you did the first time around. In most cases, a microwave does this best—retaining most of the taste and texture of the original.

Don't bother to heat them up. Discover how the flavor of a hot food changes when it's cold. Cold leftover pizza actually makes a good, quick breakfast.

Make a sandwich out of it. Meat loaf, chicken, meatballs, pot roast—these all make an excellent sandwich if you slice them thin enough, and add some lettuce, tomato, onion, pickle, mayonnaise, mustard, etc., etc., etc. Certain persons even claim that leftover spaghetti makes a great sandwich, but this has not been confirmed.

Give it another life altogether. Reincarnate those potatoes as a potato salad. Turn those leftover vegetables into soup. Help those shreds of chicken or turkey to return as a stir-fry. Create a brand-new dinner from old food—you *can* make a silk purse out of a sow's ear. Or, at the very least, a casserole.

Fried Rice with Whatever

Fried rice—a brilliant invention—is at its best when made with leftover rice and whatever bits of stuff you happen to have in your fridge. Vegetarians can just skip the meat and double the vegetables.

2 tbsp (30 mL)	vegetable oil
1	onion, chopped
2	cloves garlic, squished
1	egg, beaten
2 cups (500 mL)	diced raw or cooked vegetables—any mixture of whatever you have around—celery, green pepper, mushrooms, carrots, bean sprouts, green beans, broccoli, zucchini, peas
2 cups (500 mL)	diced cooked meat or fish, any kind (chicken, beef, pork, shrimp, turkey, groundhog, etc.)
3 cups (750 mL)	leftover rice
2 tbsp (30 mL)	soy sauce
1 tsp (5 mL)	sesame oil (if you have it—it's very nice)
4	green onions, sliced

In a wok or a large skillet, heat the oil over high heat and stir-fry the chopped onion and garlic for 2 or 3 minutes, just until the onion is slightly softened. Stir in the egg, and cook the mixture just until the egg is scrambled—this will only take a minute. Throw in the vegetables—whatever you're using—adding the ones that take the longest time to cook first, then the next, and the next, and the next, adding any cooked vegetables at the last minute. Generally, soft watery vegetables (like zucchini and bean sprouts) will cook faster than hard, solid ones (like carrots and celery). But really, don't go all technical about this, it isn't astrophysics, just dinner.

When the vegetables are all in the wok, throw in the meat, and stir it around a bit. Since it's already cooked, it will just need to be heated. Now add the rice, and keep stirring. Add the soy sauce, and cook the whole business together, stirring and tossing, for 2 or 3 minutes, until everything is hot and well mixed. Sprinkle in the sesame oil, if you're using it, and the green onions, toss it all around, and remove from heat.

Serves 3 or 4 as a main dish.

Dribs and Drabs Stir-Fry

This is not a recipe. Well, not exactly. Only you know what dribs and drabs lurk in the darkest recesses of your refrigerator. Half a withered onion. Two pitiful carrots. A pathetic, lonesome, partially eaten chicken leg. Seven green beans (why did you keep seven green beans?). This sorry collection is about to turn into dinner. Really.

Start by cutting up everything you can find into smallish pieces. Arrange these attractively on a large platter (or a couple of plates). Put all the cooked stuff (leftover pot roast, yesterday's broccoli, half a can of corn niblets) together on one plate since these won't require as much stir-frying as the raw stuff (hunk of green pepper, slab of cabbage, sliver of bacon). It's already starting to feel like something, isn't it?

Now make up a sauce. In a small bowl, stir together 2 tsp (10 mL) cornstarch, 2 tbsp (30 mL) soy sauce, and ½ cup (125 mL) water, broth, or vegetable juice (like the liquid from a can of peas or something).

OK. Start frying. Heat 2 tbsp (30 mL) of vegetable oil in a wok or a large skillet over high heat. Definitely throw in some chopped or sliced onion to start. This always smells productive. Now add the raw stuff— meat first, if you've got some, then the hard vegetables (like carrots), then the softer things (like mushrooms). Stir-fry, tossing constantly, until the meat is cooked and the vegetables are looking hopeful. Now add the cooked bits, a little at a time until everything is in, and stir-fry for a couple of minutes more.

Now, stir up the sauce mixture (the cornstarch will have settled to the bottom of the bowl) and add it, all at once, to the skillet. Cook, stirring constantly, for about a minute, until slightly thickened and bubbly. Remove from the heat and serve over hot cooked rice or pasta.

Wow. And you thought there was nothing good in the house to eat.

Primarily Pasta

Pasta Basics

Just exactly how much pasta is too much? Or worse, how much is too little? And how do you cook the stuff?

For one serving:

Long pasta, like spaghetti, fettuccine and the like:	¾-inch (2-cm) diameter bunch
Regular-size macaroni, like elbows, small shells, fusilli:	1 cup (250 mL)
Larger macaroni like rotini, large shells, rigatoni:	1⅔ cup (400 mL)
Noodles—fine, medium, and wide:	1⅔ cup (400 mL)

Shortcut:

Macaroni will expand to double in volume when cooked. So if you think you can eat a whole bowlful of macaroni, fill it halfway with the dry pasta and it should end up being about right.

Cooking the stuff:

Fill your largest pot with water, and bring it to a full boil over high heat. If you cover the pot while it's heating, the water will boil faster. Add the pasta to the boiling water—it will stop boiling temporarily as the pasta lowers the temperature of the water. Stir until the water returns to a boil, then cook the pasta until done, stirring just occasionally. *Don't cover the pot.*

How can you tell when it's done?

Small, thin pasta will cook more quickly than big fat pasta. Start tasting after 5 minutes. It should be tender, but still a little chewy through the middle (in Italian this is called *al dente*, meaning "to the tooth"). If you are cooking spaghetti, you can use the ever-popular Wall Test: throw a strand against the wall and if it sticks, it's done. (This test is not recommended, however, for stucco walls.)

Drain the pasta thoroughly in a strainer or colander and dump it immediately into a serving bowl or back into the cooking pot to toss with your sauce. *Do not rinse the cooked pasta unless you are planning to use it in another recipe, like pasta salad, or a macaroni casserole.*

Pasta Trivia:

Adding a spoonful of oil to the cooking water does absolutely nothing useful, no matter what anyone tells you. It does not prevent the pasta from sticking together, and it does not prevent the pot from boiling over. Better to just avoid overcooking, and keep an eye on the stove.

Salt doesn't help the water boil faster. No. It does make the water a little salty, and if that's what you want, go ahead and add it. But otherwise, you can just add salt when you're saucing the pasta.

If your pot starts to boil over, just blow hard over the surface and it will settle down. Meanwhile lower the heat to keep it from happening again.

Don't get stuck in a pasta rut. Elbows and spaghetti aren't the only things out there, you know. Have you ever tried fusilli? Or radiatore? Or farfalle? Each shape tastes different. Really.

Big Batch Spaghetti Sauce

Every summer, millions of innocent tomatoes are left to wither and rot simply because they have no one to love and take care of them. This senseless waste must stop! Go seek out a big basket of perfectly ripe tomatoes, bring them home, and make a year's worth of spaghetti sauce.

¼ cup (50 mL)	olive or vegetable oil
2	onions, chopped
4 to 6	cloves garlic, squished
12 cups (3 L)	chopped ripe tomatoes
2 tbsp (30 mL)	tomato paste
1 tsp (5 mL)	salt
½ tsp (2 mL)	pepper
½ cup (125 mL)	chopped fresh herbs (parsley, basil, oregano, whatever) *or*
1 tbsp (15 mL)	*each* dried basil and oregano

In your largest pot, heat the oil and sauté the onion and garlic over medium heat for 5 to 7 minutes, until softened. Dump in the chopped tomatoes, and bring to a boil, stirring often. Add the tomato paste, the salt and pepper, and leave the whole business to simmer (no lid) for about an hour, stirring once in a while.

When the sauce is nearly thick enough, add the fresh or dried herbs, and simmer for another 15 minutes or so. Your homemade sauce may not be as thick as store-bought spaghetti sauce—after all, you aren't using any starches or thickeners. You can add a little more tomato paste if you really think your sauce is too thin.

Use this sauce immediately over pasta or in lasagna, or pack into plastic containers and freeze.

Yes! You can double or triple this recipe if you want to! Just remember, the bigger the batch, the longer the cooking time.

Chopping tomatoes

The fastest way to chop up a bunch of ripe tomatoes is to put them in a big bowl and mush them up with your bare hands. Just dive in there and squish away to your heart's content. Totally gross, very effective, really fun.

Bolognese Sauce

What's with the fancy name, you ask? Heck, this is just regular spaghetti sauce with meat, you say? Well, whatever.

1 tbsp (15 mL)	**vegetable or olive oil**
1	**medium onion, chopped**
1	**medium carrot, chopped**
1	**stalk celery, chopped**
1 cup (250 mL)	**chicken broth**
½ lb (250 g)	**medium ground beef or ground turkey**
⅓ cup (60 mL)	**tomato paste**
1⅔ cups (400 mL)	**milk**
½ tsp (2 mL)	**oregano**
	salt and pepper to taste
¼ cup (50 mL)	**Parmesan cheese**

Heat the oil in a large skillet. Add the onion and cook, stirring, over medium heat for about 5 minutes, until softened. Add the carrot, the celery and *half* of the chicken broth, and cook for about 5 minutes, until the vegetables are tender.

Add the ground beef or turkey and cook, stirring to break up the lumps, until the meat is no longer pink—about 5 minutes. Pour in the rest of the chicken broth, and cook just until the liquid has nearly all evaporated—about 4 minutes. Now add the tomato paste, *half* of the milk, the oregano, and some salt and pepper, and simmer until the milk has mostly evaporated, then add the rest of the milk and cook over low heat, stirring, for about 20 minutes. The sauce should be creamy and thickened.

Serve over hot, cooked pasta (rotini is good for this sort of sauce), sprinkled with the Parmesan cheese.

Makes enough sauce for 4 servings of pasta.

Chicken and Mushroom Pasta

You can save time by buying skinless and boneless chicken thighs, or you can save money by doing it all yourself. You decide.

2 lbs (1 kg)	chicken thighs—*with* skin and bone (about 1 lb/500 g prepared meat)
1 tbsp (15 mL)	vegetable oil
1	onion, chopped
1½ cups (375 mL)	sliced mushrooms
1 19-oz (540 mL)	can *stewed* tomatoes
1 cup (250 mL)	water
1 tsp (5 mL)	dried basil (or 1 tbsp/15 mL chopped fresh basil, if you have it)
2 cups (500 mL)	smallish pasta—shells, bow ties, fusilli, elbows salt and pepper to taste

Skin the chicken thighs, remove the bones, and cut the meat into (more or less) ½-inch (1 cm) pieces. Don't worry about getting the pieces all the same size or anything. Just cut it off the bones however it comes. Discard the skin and bones (or save them for making soup).

Heat the vegetable oil in a large skillet, add the chicken pieces, and cook over medium high heat until the meat is no longer pink—about 5 to 7 minutes. Remove the meat from the skillet, leaving as much of the oil in the pan as possible.

Add the onion and mushrooms to the skillet and cook over medium heat until softened, about 5 minutes. Pour in the stewed tomatoes, the water and the basil, bring to a boil, then add the (uncooked) pasta, cover with a lid, and cook over low heat for 8 to 10 minutes, until the pasta is done, stirring once in a while.

Return the chicken to the pan and cook for about 5 minutes, until the mixture is completely heated through. Season with salt and pepper.

Makes about 4 servings.

Spicy Peanut Chicken Pasta

Go ahead and add more stuff to this, if you want—canned baby corn, fresh snow peas, some bean sprouts, almost anything.

2 lbs (1 kg)	chicken thighs—*with* skin and bones (about 1 lb/500 g prepared meat)
1 tbsp (15 mL)	vegetable oil
1 cup (250 mL)	chicken broth (homemade, canned, or from bouillon powder or cube)
2 tbsp (30 mL)	honey
1 tbsp (15 mL)	soy sauce
¼ cup (50 mL)	peanut butter—smooth or chunky
1 tbsp (15 mL)	cornstarch
1 tsp (5 mL)	ground ginger
½ tsp (2 mL)	hot pepper flakes (or more, or less, or whatever)
2	green onions, sliced
2	cloves garlic, squished
1	green or red pepper, thinly sliced

Skin the chicken thighs, remove the bones, and cut the meat up into ½-inch (1 cm) pieces. (Don't measure, just cut it up however it comes off the bone.) Discard the skin and bones, or save them for soup.

Heat the vegetable oil in a large skillet, add the chicken chunks and cook them over high heat until lightly browned—5 to 7 minutes. Remove the chicken from the pan.

In a bowl, whisk together the chicken broth, honey, soy sauce, peanut butter, cornstarch, ginger, and hot pepper flakes. Pour this mixture into the skillet and cook, stirring constantly, until thickened and smooth. Add the green onions, garlic, and green or red pepper, and cook for another couple of minutes. Return the chicken pieces (and any juice from it) to the pan and simmer the mixture for 2 or 3 minutes, until heated through.

Serve over hot, cooked pasta—thin spaghetti or linguine is good.

Makes enough for 4 servings of pasta.

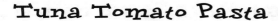
Tuna Tomato Pasta

Cheap, delicious, and much better than a tuna sandwich for dinner.

3	cloves garlic, squished
2 tbsp (30 mL)	olive oil
1 28-oz (796 mL)	can tomatoes
1 6½-oz (184 g)	can tuna, drained
½ tsp (2 mL)	dried oregano
½ tsp (2 mL)	dried basil
½ tsp (2 mL)	red pepper flakes
½ tsp (2 mL)	salt
1 tbsp (15 mL)	capers (optional, but nice, if you have them)

In a large skillet, sauté the garlic in the olive oil for a couple of minutes, until softened. Dump in the tomatoes, juice and all, and mash them up with a fork or a potato masher. Add the tuna, seasonings, and capers, and stir. Bring to a boil, then lower the heat, and simmer for about 15 minutes.

Toss with hot cooked pasta and sprinkle with lots of grated Parmesan cheese.

Makes enough sauce for 4 servings of pasta.

Basically Garlic Tomato Sauce

Nothing in the house to eat? Think again. If you have a can of tomatoes, a bit of garlic, and some pasta, you've got dinner. You can leave the parsley out, if you don't have it.

¼ cup (50 mL)	vegetable oil (or olive oil, if you can manage it)
4	cloves garlic, finely chopped
½ cup (125 mL)	chopped fresh parsley
1 28-oz (796 mL)	can plum tomatoes
	salt and pepper

Heat the oil in a medium saucepan, add the garlic, and cook it over low heat for 5 to 10 minutes, until very soft but not brown. Add half the parsley and cook, stirring, for another 5 minutes.

Pour in the entire can of tomatoes including all the juice, squishing them with a wooden spoon to break them up. Now let this simmer over medium low heat, for a long time—maybe half an hour to 45 minutes, stirring once in a while. The sauce should thicken slowly, but still be a little lumpy. When you think it's just about done, add the rest of the parsley, and some salt and pepper to taste.

Toss with hot, drained spaghetti or fettuccine. A sprinkle of cheese is nice.

Makes enough sauce for 4 servings of pasta.

Eggplant Pasta Sauce

Eggplants are mysterious. Deep. Inscrutable. Make this dish and you will be, too. Really.

1	medium eggplant
1 tsp (5 mL)	salt
¼ cup (50 mL)	vegetable or olive oil
1	large onion, chopped
2	cloves garlic, squished
6	medium tomatoes, canned or fresh
1 tsp (5 mL)	sugar
1 tbsp (15 mL)	chopped fresh parsley
1 tbsp (15 mL)	chopped fresh basil (or 1 tsp/5 mL dried)

Peel the eggplant and cut it into ½-inch (1 cm) cubes. Place in a colander or strainer over a bowl, and sprinkle with salt. Let drain for an hour or so. This removes some of the excess water from the eggplant so that it cooks faster and doesn't absorb as much oil. Pat the cubes dry with paper towel.

Heat half of the oil in a large skillet, add the eggplant cubes, and cook, stirring, over medium high heat, until golden—5 to 7 minutes. Remove from the pan. Add the rest of the oil to the pan, and cook the onion and garlic for 5 minutes, until soft. Return the eggplant to the skillet, and add the tomatoes, sugar, parsley, and basil. Lower the heat, and simmer for about 10 minutes.

Makes enough sauce for 4 servings of pasta.

Rotini with Broccoli

Fast, delicious and, when broccoli is seventy-nine cents a bunch, a very cheap dinner.

4 cups (1 L)	uncooked rotini (or similar) pasta
1	bunch broccoli, stalks peeled and sliced and top cut into flowerets
2 tbsp (30 mL)	vegetable or olive oil
4	cloves garlic, squished
2 cups (500 mL)	diced tomatoes (fresh or canned)
¼ cup (50 mL)	chopped fresh parsley
½ cup (125 mL)	grated Parmesan cheese
	salt and pepper to taste

Cook the rotini in plenty of boiling water until done. Drain and rinse under running water to prevent it from sticking together. Set aside.

In a steamer (or in a colander) over boiling water, cook the broccoli until just tender but still slightly crisp—7 to 10 minutes. As soon as it's done, remove from the steamer and set aside.

Heat the oil in a large skillet and sauté the garlic for 2 minutes, just until softened. Add the tomatoes and parsley, and cook for 5 minutes. Throw in the broccoli, and toss around for a couple of minutes, until it's heated through. Stir in the rotini and the Parmesan cheese, season with salt and pepper, and serve immediately.

Makes 4 servings.

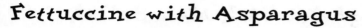
Fettuccine with Asparagus

This is where asparagus wants to go when it dies. Asparagus nirvana. Save this great recipe for a special occasion.

½ cup (125 mL)	butter
¼ cup (50 mL)	whipping cream
1 cup (250 mL)	grated Parmesan cheese
1 lb (500 g)	asparagus, trimmed and cut in 1-inch (2 cm) pieces (on the diagonal is classy)
3 tbsp (45 mL)	butter
2	green onions, sliced
1 lb (500 g)	fettuccine pasta
	salt and pepper

In a bowl, with an electric mixer, beat together the ½ cup (125 mL) of butter with the whipping cream until just fluffy. Beat in the Parmesan cheese, a little at a time. Set aside.

Steam the asparagus for 5 to 7 minutes, until just turning bright green. Remove from heat and place under cold running water to stop the asparagus from overcooking. Set aside.

Melt the 3 tbsp (45 mL) of butter in a skillet, and add the green onion, stirring over medium heat for 2 minutes. Toss in the asparagus, and let it cook for just a minute more, until hot.

Cook the fettuccine, drain it thoroughly, and return it to the pot (not on the heat). Add the butter/Parmesan cheese mixture by spoonfuls, stirring until melted into a creamy sauce, then dump in the asparagus, and toss until combined. Add salt and pepper to taste.

Makes 4 incredible servings.

Spaghetti with Meatballs

A red-and-white-checkered tablecloth. A wine bottle with a candle stuck in it. A basket of garlic bread. Spaghetti and meatballs. A classic.

2 tbsp (30 mL)	vegetable or olive oil
½ cup (125 mL)	chopped onion
2	cloves garlic, squished
½ cup (125 mL)	chopped green pepper
½ cup (125 mL)	sliced mushrooms
1 28-oz (796 mL)	can plain spaghetti sauce (or *about* 4 cups homemade sauce)
½ tsp (2 mL)	oregano
½ tsp (2 mL)	basil
1 batch	Plain Old Meatballs, cooked (recipe on page 70)

Heat the vegetable oil in a large saucepan or skillet over medium heat. Add the chopped onion and the garlic, and cook for 2 minutes, until just softened. Now, add the green peppers and sliced mushrooms, and cook for another 2 or 3 minutes. Pour in the spaghetti sauce, oregano, and basil, and just heat to a simmer.

Plunk the Plain Old Meatballs into the simmering sauce and cook, stirring occasionally, for 20 to 30 minutes.

Serve over hot cooked spaghetti, sprinkled with grated Parmesan cheese. Makes about 4 servings.

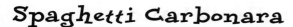
Spaghetti Carbonara

This pasta dish cooks in the time it takes to boil the spaghetti. No one will believe it when they find out how you made it. Maybe you shouldn't tell them.

½ lb (250 g)	spaghetti
6	slices bacon, chopped into little pieces
½ tsp (2 mL)	red pepper flakes (optional, but good)
2	eggs, beaten
½ cup (125 mL)	grated Parmesan cheese
	salt and pepper to taste

Fill a big pot almost to the top with water, and bring it to a boil over high heat. Carefully add the spaghetti to the pot, keeping the water boiling, and stir with a wooden spoon to make sure the strands don't clump together.

While the spaghetti is cooking, fry the bacon in a small skillet with the red pepper flakes, until crisp but not incinerated. Tip the skillet gently and pour the fat out into an empty can (*not down the drain!!!*). Set it aside.

When the spaghetti is done (throw a strand against the wall, and if it sticks, it's cooked) drain it in a colander but *don't rinse it.* Dump the spaghetti into a large bowl, and *immediately* toss it with the *raw* beaten eggs (yes, really), the cooked bacon, and the Parmesan cheese. Stir it all together well. I promise you, this is not disgusting. The heat of the spaghetti actually cooks the eggs, and the whole thing combines into a delicious, creamy sauce.

Season with salt and pepper and serve right away—pronto.

This makes 2 servings, but you can double the recipe to serve more people.

Pasta with Pesto Sauce

This may seem like a strange recipe—it's not actually cooked; it's green; it's weird. It's amazing.

½ cup (125 mL)	olive oil
¼ cup (50 mL)	pine nuts (or almonds, but pine nuts are better)
2 cups (500 mL)	fresh basil leaves, firmly packed into the measuring cup
2	cloves garlic (or more, if you're that type of person)
½ tsp (2 mL)	salt
¾ cup (175 mL)	grated Parmesan cheese (*freshly* grated, if possible)

Pour about a tablespoon (15 mL) of the olive oil into a small skillet. Add the pine nuts (or almonds) and heat *very gently*, stirring constantly for about 3 minutes, until the nuts are lightly browned. Watch this like a hawk because you don't want to burn these, as pine nuts cost about the same as a small car. Set aside to cool.

Stuff the basil leaves, pine nuts, garlic, salt, and all the remaining olive oil into the container of a food processor or a blender. Blend until almost smooth, scraping the sides down several times, so that it blends evenly. A little texture is okay, but no big leafy clumps, please. Scoop this into a bowl and stir in the Parmesan cheese.

Now cook your pasta in the usual way, drain it (don't rinse!!!), and dump it back into the pot (not on the stove). Stir in the pesto sauce, tossing everything around so that it coats the pasta evenly. Scoop into a serving dish, and serve immediately.

Makes 4 servings.

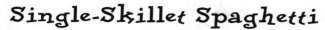

Single-Skillet Spaghetti

*How can you not love a recipe that leaves you with just a single
frying pan to wash?*

1 lb (500 g)	lean ground beef, ground turkey, or ground chicken
2 cups (500 mL)	sliced mushrooms
1 cup (250 mL)	chopped onion
1 cup (250 mL)	chopped green pepper
1 28-oz (796 mL)	can tomatoes
1 cup (250 mL)	water
1½ cups (375 mL)	broken *raw* spaghetti strands
1 tsp (5 mL)	oregano
1 tsp (5 mL)	salt
2 cups (500 mL)	shredded cheese (mozzarella, cheddar, or whatever)

In a large skillet, combine the beef (or whatever meat you're using),
mushrooms, onions, and green pepper. Sauté over medium heat until
the meat is browned and the vegetables are tender. Drain off any fat
that might collect into an empty can or bowl—not down the sink.

Dump in the can of tomatoes (with all the juice), mashing them up
a bit with your spoon. Stir in the water, spaghetti, oregano, and salt.
Bring to a boil, then reduce the heat, cover, and simmer for 15 to 20
minutes, until the spaghetti is cooked.

Remove from heat, stir in the cheese, and serve.

Makes 4 to 5 servings.

To-Die-For Lasagna

The genius who invented no-boil lasagna noodles deserves a medal.
Eliminating the annoying noodle-cooking step was a great leap
forward in lasagna evolution.

The meat sauce

1	onion, chopped
2	cloves garlic, squished
1 lb (500 g)	medium ground beef or ground turkey (see below for vegetarian version)
1	carrot, diced
1	green pepper, diced
1 28-oz (796 mL)	can spaghetti sauce, the plain cheap kind (or *about* 4 cups [1 L] homemade spaghetti sauce)
1 cup (250 mL)	water
1 tsp (5 mL)	oregano

The filling, etc.

2 cups (500 mL)	ricotta or cottage cheese
2	eggs
2 tbsp (30 mL)	chopped fresh parsley (if you have it)
3 cups (750 mL)	grated mozzarella cheese
¼ cup (50 mL)	grated Parmesan cheese
15	no-boil oven-ready lasagna noodles

Preheat the oven to 350° F (180° C).

In a large skillet or Dutch oven, combine the onions, garlic, and ground meat, and cook over medium heat until the meat is no longer pink, stirring to break up lumps. Add the carrot and green pepper and cook for 5 minutes longer. Drain off the fat by pouring or spooning it into an empty can. Add the spaghetti sauce, water, and oregano, and cook, stirring once in a while, for 15 minutes, or until the carrots are tender.

Mix together the ricotta or cottage cheese, the eggs, and the parsley in a small bowl. Have everything else ready to go.

Spread about 1 cup (250 mL) of the meat sauce on the bottom of a 9 × 13-inch (22 × 33 cm) baking dish. It won't quite cover the bottom, but that's OK. Arrange 5 of the lasagna noodles on the sauce, covering the entire bottom of the baking dish, with just a bit of space between them. You may need to break one of the noodles so that the whole business fits together right. Cover the noodles with 2 cups (500 mL) of meat sauce, spoon on ½ of the ricotta mixture, then sprinkle with 1 cup (250 mL) of the mozzarella cheese. Now, again: 5 more noodles, 2 cups of meat sauce, the rest of the ricotta, and another cup (250 mL) of the mozzarella. Are you still with me?

Finally, put the last 5 lasagna noodles on top, spread all the rest of the meat sauce over it, and sprinkle on the rest of the mozzarella and all of the Parmesan cheese. Whew.

Cover the baking dish loosely with foil (try not to let the foil touch the cheese) and bake at 350° F (180° C) for 30 minutes. Remove the foil and bake for another 15 minutes, until the sauce is bubbling and the lasagna noodles are tender (poke a knife into the middle to make sure).

Makes 8-ish servings.

Vegetarian Alert! Yes, you too can make To-Die-For Lasagna. Instead of the ground beef, sauté 1 cup (250 mL) chopped mushrooms, and 1 cup (250 mL) diced zucchini with the onions and garlic at the beginning of the recipe. Then, add 2 cups (500 mL) chopped raw spinach to the sauce about 5 minutes before it's finished cooking.

Macaroni and Cheese Not from a Box

There are times when you want macaroni and cheese from a box. At such a time, this recipe will simply not do. But there are times when you want the other kind. The kind with lots of real cheese, and a crispy top—the kind that takes more than seven minutes to make. This is it. And it is good.

3 cups (750 mL)	elbow macaroni, uncooked
	one *double recipe* Basic White Sauce (see page 115)
3 cups (750 mL)	grated cheddar cheese
1 cup (250 mL)	soft bread crumbs
2 tbsp (30 mL)	butter, melted

Preheat the oven to 350° F (180° C).

Cook the macaroni in lots of boiling water until well done. Really well done. *Not al dente*. Drain and rinse with cold water.

While the macaroni is cooking, make a *double recipe* (this means you should double the amounts of all the ingredients—got it?) of white sauce, adding just a bit of salt and pepper—*nothing else*. Remove from heat and add the grated cheese, stirring until all the cheese is melted and the sauce is nice and smooth and goopy.

Combine the cooked macaroni with the cheese sauce and turn it into a greased 2- or 3-quart (2 or 3 liter) ovenproof casserole.

Mix together the bread crumbs with the melted butter and sprinkle this on top of the macaroni.

Bake at 350° F (180° C) for 30 to 40 minutes, until the sauce is bubbly and the topping is crisp and golden. You can, if you must, eat this with ketchup.

Makes 6 servings, or thereabouts.

Basic White Sauce

Everyone should know how to make a basic white sauce. You will get endless mileage out of this recipe, and your friends will think you're brilliant. You can add some chopped herbs to this, if you like, or grated cheese to make it into cheese sauce.

2 tbsp (30 mL)	butter or margarine
2 tbsp (30 mL)	flour
1 cup (250 mL)	milk
	salt and pepper to taste

In a small saucepan, over low heat, melt the butter. Add the flour stirring it thoroughly into the butter. Cook, very gently, for a couple of minutes. Now, slowly stir in the milk. First the mixture will be lumpy, but as you stir it over the heat, it will become smooth and begin to thicken. Continue cooking the sauce over low heat for at least 5 minutes after it has thickened, but keep stirring so that the bottom doesn't burn and stick.

Now, season the sauce with salt and pepper—a little at a time until it tastes right. If you're using herbs, add them now. If you want to add cheese, take the sauce *off the heat*, and stir in about half a cup of grated cheese (any kind you like), whisking until it's smooth and melted. Don't cook the sauce after you've added the cheese or it will get stringy.

Makes about 1 cup (250 mL) of white sauce, more if you add cheese to it.

Extraordinary Eggs

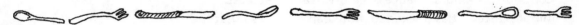

When all else fails, eat eggs. They're delicious, fast to cook, and a good source of protein. If you turn a few eggs into a dish with a foreign name, no one will suspect you're eating them because they're cheap. Not even you.

Outrageous Omelets

An omelet is nothing more than a scrambled egg pancake with a filling. The trick of it is to cook the egg so it isn't rubbery, and to get it out of the pan in one piece. No big deal, once you get the hang of it. And even your failures can be served as scrambled eggs.

3	eggs
1 tbsp (15 mL)	water
1 tbsp (15 mL)	butter
	salt and pepper
	filling (see below for ideas)

In a small bowl, beat the eggs with the water until bubbly.

In a medium (10-inch/25 cm) skillet, heat the butter over medium heat until foamy. Pour the eggs into the pan, and let them cook undisturbed over medium-low heat for a minute. As the egg begins to set, gently lift the edges with a spatula and allow the uncooked parts to run underneath. Keep doing this until the egg is cooked, but still moist on top. (This takes a bit of practice to get just right.) Sprinkle with salt and pepper and remove from heat.

Now, spoon your filling onto one half of the omelet, flip the unfilled side over to cover the filling, and slide the whole thing out onto a plate. Serve immediately.

Voilà! An outrageous omelet for one.

Outrageous Omelet fillings (prepare this before you start cooking the eggs):

- Diced cooked (leftover?) potato sautéed with onion and chopped bacon
- Chopped ham and Swiss cheese
- Spaghetti sauce and mozzarella cheese
- Mushrooms sautéed with onions
- Sautéed green pepper, onion, and tomato
- Diced apples sautéed in butter with cinnamon and sugar
- Any old leftover vegetables, chopped up and sautéed with some green onion and, maybe, some cheese

Unfettered Frittatas

A frittata is basically an omelet, only easier. It is made of the same stuff, but it doesn't require any finicky messing around or fancy folding during the cooking process.

¼ cup (50 mL)	olive or vegetable oil
1	medium onion, thinly sliced
1½ cups (375 mL)	any sliced or diced vegetable, raw or cooked (mushrooms, zucchini, green beans, peppers, potato, spinach—*anything*)
6	eggs, beaten
¼ cup (50 mL)	grated Parmesan cheese
	salt, pepper, and any herbs or spices that you want to use
2 tbsp (30 mL)	butter

Heat the olive or vegetable oil in a 10-inch (25 cm) skillet, add the sliced onion and sauté for about 5 minutes, until softened. Throw in whatever vegetables you're using, and cook them with the onion. Raw vegetables will, naturally, require more cooking than ones that are already cooked, so pay attention. Sauté raw veggies until they're tender. Cooked ones should just be stirred around a bit.

Scoop the onion-vegetable mixture into the bowl with the beaten eggs, along with about half of the Parmesan cheese, some salt and pepper and whatever herbs or spices you're using. Stir to mix, and set aside.

Melt the 2 tbsp (30 mL) of butter in the same skillet (the one you cooked the onions etc. in, which should now be empty). Heat it over medium heat just until it begins to get foamy, then pour in the egg/vegetable mixture. Lower the heat immediately to *very low*, and cook the frittata for 15 to 20 minutes, just until the eggs have set. They'll still be a little wobbly in the middle—that's OK.

Preheat the broiler element of your oven. Sprinkle the top of the frittata with the rest of the Parmesan cheese, then slide the pan onto the highest rack of the oven for about a minute, until the top is set and lightly browned. *Very* lightly browned.

Loosen the edges of the frittata by running a knife around the pan, slide the frittata out onto a serving plate and cut into wedges to serve.

Makes 3 or 4 servings.

Quirky Quiches

Fancy cousin to the frittata, with a certain Omelet Family resemblance. If you use a frozen ready-to-bake pastry shell, you can throw a quiche together in about fifteen minutes. If you make your own pastry (page 159) it'll take a few minutes more.

2 tbsp (30 mL)	butter, margarine, or vegetable oil
½ cup (125 mL)	chopped onion
1½ cups (375 mL)	any sliced or diced vegetable, raw or cooked (mushrooms, zucchini, green beans, peppers, potato, spinach—*anything*)
½ lb (250 g)	shredded cheese (Swiss, cheddar, Monterey Jack—any kind except the processed cheese-slice kind)—about ½ cup/125 mL
3	eggs
1 cup (250 mL)	milk or plain yogurt
¼ tsp (1 mL)	salt
	pepper to taste

Preheat the oven to 375° F (190° C).

First, get your crust ready. If you're using your own pastry, line a 9-inch (22 cm) pie pan with rolled pastry dough, crimping up the edges to make it frilly. If you're using a ready-made crust, take it out of the freezer, and have it ready to fill.

Melt the butter or margarine (or heat the vegetable oil) in a large skillet, and sauté the onion over medium heat for about 5 minutes, until soft. Add the sliced or diced vegetables and cook for a few minutes. If you're using raw vegetables, cook them just until they're softened. If you're using vegetables that are already cooked, they'll just need to be sautéed for a minute or so, to wake them up a bit. Let this mixture cool for a couple of minutes, then spread it in the bottom of the pastry crust. Sprinkle the shredded cheese evenly over the vegetables.

In a small bowl, beat the eggs together with the milk or yogurt and the salt. Add some pepper if you like, and anything else that might fit your mood (oregano? paprika? cayenne? basil?). Pour over the cheese and vegetables.

Bake the quiche at 375° F (190° C) for 35 to 40 minutes, until puffed and golden, and a knife poked into the middle comes out clean(ish).

Makes about 4 servings.

Scrambled Pepper Eggs

A couple of peppers, a lone leftover potato, some eggs. Dinner.
In fifteen minutes.

2 tbsp (30 mL)	**butter**
1	**onion, chopped**
2	**medium green peppers, diced (want to throw in a hot one?)**
1	**cooked potato, peeled and diced**
8	**eggs**
½ tsp (2 mL)	**salt**
¼ tsp (1 mL)	**pepper**

Melt 1 tbsp (15 mL) of the butter in a medium skillet, add the onion and peppers and sauté over medium heat for 8 to 10 minutes, until softened. Add the potato and continue cooking for 5 minutes. Dump into a bowl.

Beat the eggs with the salt and pepper. Melt the remaining 1 tbsp (15 mL) of butter in the skillet, over medium heat. Pour in the eggs and cook, stirring, until almost set—about 2 minutes. Stir in the pepper mixture, and serve immediately.

Makes 4 servings.

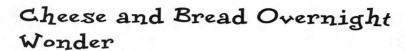

Cheese and Bread Overnight Wonder

There's nothing good left to eat in the house. Nothing. Just some stale old bread. A hunk of cheese. A few eggs, some milk, a shriveled tomato. Can you wait a few hours?

16	slices of bread, any kind—fresh, stale, whatever
1 lb (500 g)	shredded cheese, any kind (a mixture is fine)
4	green onions, chopped
5	eggs, beaten
3 cups (750 mL)	milk
1 tbsp (15 mL)	mustard (Dijon, if you have it)
1 tsp (5 mL)	salt
¼ tsp (1 mL)	ground cayenne pepper
1 or 2	tomatoes, sliced
⅓ cup (75 mL)	grated Parmesan cheese
2 tbsp (30 mL)	butter, cut in bits

Preheat the oven to 350° F (180° C).

In a well-greased 3-quart (3 liter) baking dish (any shape) arrange the following layers: first, a layer of bread, then a handful of shredded cheese, and then a sprinkle of green onions. Repeat these layers 2 more times, making a total of 3 layers of each, ending with the green onions.

In a bowl, mix together the beaten eggs, the milk, the mustard, the salt, and the cayenne. Pour this business over the dish, cover with plastic wrap, and refrigerate for several hours or overnight. Or longer. It really doesn't matter.

When you're ready to cook, remove the plastic, arrange the tomato slices artistically on top, and sprinkle with Parmesan cheese and some butter bits.

Bake at 350° F (180° C) for 50 to 60 minutes, until puffed in the middle and a knife poked into it comes out clean.

Makes 4 to 6 servings, depending on how hungry you are.

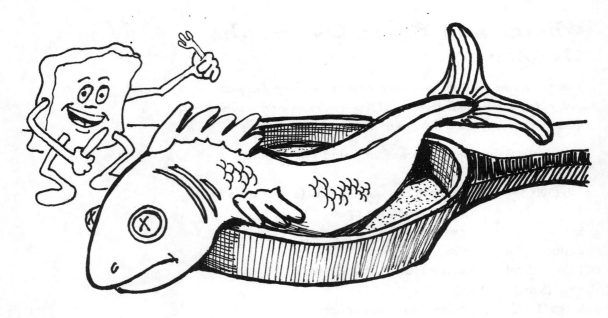

Something Fishy

Fish à la Foil

How could you not love a recipe that leaves you with no pan to wash?

1½ lbs (750 g)	fish fillets, any kind
¼ cup (50 mL)	butter, melted
2 tbsp (30 mL)	chopped parsley
1 tbsp (15 mL)	lemon juice
1 tsp (5 mL)	salt
1	small onion, very thinly sliced
2	medium carrots, coarsely grated
1 cup (250 mL)	shredded Swiss or cheddar cheese

Defrost the fish thoroughly, if you're using frozen, and divide it roughly into four serving-size portions. In a small bowl, combine the butter, parsley, lemon juice, and salt. Arrange the onion, carrot, and cheese in separate small bowls. And, finally, cut four 12-inch (20 cm) squares of heavy-duty aluminum foil.

Preheat the oven to 450° F (230° C).

Spread about a tablespoon (15 mL) of the parsley mixture onto the middle of square of foil. Top this with a serving of fish. Add a few onion rings, sprinkle with some shredded carrot, and then some shredded cheese. Exactly how much of any ingredient to include in any particular packet is up to you. If there is any of the parsley mixture left at the end, add a little more of it to each serving. Fold the foil up, forming a secure seal on top and sides.

Place the packets on a baking sheet, and bake at 450° F (230° C) for 20 to 25 minutes.

Remove packets from the oven, place one on each plate, and allow each eater to peel open his or her own. Surprise!

Makes 4 serving-size packets.

Potato-Chip-Encrusted Fish

Absolutely juvenile! Totally unsophisticated! Very delicious.

½ cup (125 mL)	Italian vinaigrette salad dressing (homemade or bottled)
1½ lbs (750 mL)	fish fillets
3 cups (750 mL)	potato chips
1 cup (250 mL)	shredded cheddar cheese

Preheat the oven to 400° F (200° C).

Pour salad dressing into a flattish bowl. Dip each fillet into the dressing, coating both sides, then arrange in a single layer on a greased cookie sheet.

Put the potato chips in a large, heavy-duty zip-top plastic bag, and zip it shut, leaving a tiny opening for the air to escape. Now, using a rolling pin, crush the potato chips into smithereens. Sprinkle the smithereens evenly over the fish on the baking sheet. And finally, top with the shredded cheese.

Bake at 400° F (200° C) for about 20 minutes, until fish flakes when you test it with a fork.

Serves 4.

Chowder from the Black Lagoon

If you're using frozen fish, don't even bother thawing it. Just hack it into chunks, and plunk it into the pot. Add a salad and some good bread and you've got dinner in less than half an hour.

¼ cup (50 mL)	butter
1	large onion, chopped
2	medium carrots, grated
3	medium potatoes, peeled and diced
1 tsp (5 mL)	salt
½ tsp (2 mL)	thyme
1	bay leaf
2 cups (500 mL)	milk
1 lb (500 g)	fish fillets, frozen or fresh
½ lb (250 g)	mushrooms, sliced
2 tbsp (30 mL)	chopped fresh parsley

Melt the butter in a large saucepan, then add the onion, and cook over medium heat until just softened. Toss in the carrots and potatoes, stir, then add the salt, thyme, bay leaf, and milk. Bring to a boil, then lower the heat and simmer for about 15 minutes, until the potatoes are nearly done.

Cut the fish fillets into chunks and add to the pot along with the mushrooms and the parsley. Stir to mix everything up, then bring it back to a boil and simmer for about 10 minutes, until the fish is cooked. This will be quite a thick chowder. If you want something a bit more soupy, just add another half cup (125 mL) or so of milk.

Makes about 4 servings.

Shrimp Scampi

Let's say you win the lottery. Or some wealthy relative you'd never met dies and leaves you everything. Or you rob a bank. (No—just kidding—don't do that.) Anyway, let's just suppose you want to splurge. This dish is the way to go.

½ cup (125 mL)	**butter, melted**
¼ cup (50 mL)	**olive or vegetable oil**
4	**cloves garlic, squished**
¼ cup (50 mL)	**chopped green onions**
¼ tsp (1 mL)	**paprika**
½ tsp (2 mL)	**salt**
¼ tsp (1 mL)	**pepper**
2 lbs (1 kg)	**raw shrimp, as large as you can afford, peeled**

In a bowl, stir together the butter, oil, garlic, green onions, paprika, salt, and pepper. Pour this mixture over the shrimp, and toss them until they are completely coated. Spread the shrimp out onto a cookie sheet or shallow baking pan so that they're in 1 layer.

Preheat the broiler element of your oven. When it's good and hot, place the pan with the shrimp under the broiler, as close as possible to the element. Broil 2 to 3 minutes, then flip them over, and broil another 2 minutes. Serve right away—pronto—with some rice and a salad.

Makes 4 servings. Less, if they're pigs about it.

What's All This about Shrimp?

Raw shrimp come with or without their shells on. Usually, the shells should be removed before cooking (unless you're steaming the shrimp) and most recipes will even tell you to devein them. Why? No reason. Actually, removing the black vein that runs along the back of the shrimp is done mostly for appearance. If you don't like the way the vein looks, remove it with a sharp knife before cooking. If you don't care, then just leave it in—it won't kill you.

Tunaburgers

It's summer, and you're surrounded by barbecues. The delicious smell of scorched meat fills the air. You're depressed. All you have in the house is a can of tuna. These burgers are delicious, easy to make, and will satisfy that primal need for something charred beyond recognition. Yum.

1	medium carrot, coarsely grated
1	small onion, very finely chopped
1 6½-oz (184 g)	can tuna, drained and flaked
1	egg
2 tbsp (30 mL)	mayonnaise
1½ cups (375 mL)	fresh bread crumbs
1 tsp (5 mL)	vegetable oil
	salt and pepper

In a medium bowl, mix all the ingredients together, seasoning the mixture with salt and pepper to taste. If you have a food processor, now is the time to use it. The tuna mixture should be very well mushed together or else the burgers will fall apart when you cook them. If you don't have a processor, use a fork and mash like crazy.

By hand, form the mixture into patties.

Place tunaburgers on a preheated barbecue grill, and cook over fairly high heat for about 10 minutes per side, until golden brown. Serve in a bun, with some sliced tomato, mayonnaise, and lettuce. Oh, OK, ketchup too, if it'll make you feel more normal.

If you prefer to pan-fry the tunaburgers, heat a little vegetable oil in a large skillet, and cook the patties, 10 minutes per side, until golden. Very tiny patties can be served as tuna nuggets, with dipping sauce.

Makes 3 to 4 servings.

Completely Classic Tuna Casserole

Tuna casserole is something that you should eat on a rainy day, while wearing your favorite sloppy sweatshirt and reading old Archie comics.

1 tbsp (15 mL)	butter or margarine
¼ cup (50 mL)	finely chopped onion
1 10-oz (284 mL)	can cream of mushroom soup (don't dilute it)
2 cups (500 mL)	cooked noodles
1 6½-oz (184 mL)	can flaked tuna (white or light)
¾ cup (175 mL)	crushed potato chips

Preheat the oven to 375° F (190° C).

Melt the butter in a medium saucepan, add the onions and cook over medium heat for 8 to 10 minutes, until soft. Stir in the mushroom soup, noodles, and tuna. Dump into a greased casserole dish and top with the crushed potato chips. Bake at 375° F (190° C) for 25 to 30 minutes, until bubbly.

Feeds 2 or 3 slobs, depending on how big they are.

Vehemently Vegetarian

You're a What????

So one morning you wake up and suddenly you're a vegetarian. Maybe it was that film about the endangered wolverines of Madagascar. Maybe it was a friendly cow you met at the fair. Or maybe you just suddenly decided. It doesn't really matter. You know what you're doing. Or do you?

Not eating meat is fine. Not eating a healthful diet is not fine. If you make the choice to become a vegetarian, be smart about it. Cook yourself good food, try some interesting new dishes, and no, potato chips do not count as a vegetable. Sorry.

Going Vegetarian

There are plenty of good reasons to go vegetarian, lots of bad ones, and quite a few reasons not to even consider it at all. Becoming a vegetarian does require some understanding of your nutritional needs and an open mind. Oh, and you really do have to like vegetables.

Ten pretty good reasons to go vegetarian

- You don't really like meat all that much
- You actually prefer vegetables
- You like to cook
- You'll try anything once
- You feel healthier when you eat less meat
- You are morally opposed to eating anything with a face
- You're trying to cut down on cholesterol
- You believe it's better for the environment
- You figure it's cheaper
- It's a religious thing

Ten really dumb reasons to go vegetarian

- You think it's a good way to meet guys/girls
- It's a fashion statement
- You like French fries and nachos
- You once survived on peanut butter for a whole week
- Your best friend just became a vegetarian
- You read a magazine article that said eating meat causes brain damage
- k.d. lang is one
- You'll do anything on a dare
- You want to lose weight
- You believe that giving up meat can save the ozone layer

Ten reasons not to become a vegetarian

- You really truly (deeply) love meat
- You don't particularly like to cook
- You think tofu is totally gross
- You can't imagine French fries without gravy
- You refuse to try anything you can't pronounce
- You think vegetarians are all weirdos
- You hate beans

- You know your friends would make fun of you
- Broccoli makes you sick
- You always pick all the mushrooms, green peppers, and onions off your pizza

Ten fairly normal foods you can eat instead of meat

- Bean burritos
- Grilled cheese sandwich
- Vegetarian chili
- Pizza with no meat on it
- Veggie burgers and tofu hot dogs
- Bean and vegetable soup
- Peanut butter and banana sandwich
- Eggplant parmigiana
- Felafel in a pita
- Spaghetti with tomato sauce

Ten good things to always keep in the cupboard

- Canned beans
- Eggs
- Cheese
- Peanut butter
- Tortillas
- Dried beans and lentils
- Nuts or trail mix
- Pasta
- Veggie burgers and tofu hot dogs
- Canned vegetable or lentil soup

Boring Technical Part

OK, no one except a home-ec teacher really wants to read a bunch of nutritional drivel about food groups and all that stuff. But if you've made the decision to go vegetarian, you should do your homework. So here it is. Read it and get on with life.

Vegetarian or not, your diet should include foods from each of the following four groups: grain products, vegetables and fruit, milk products and alternatives, and meat alternatives. It's the total at the end of the day that counts—not each individual meal. So, if you're a grazing sort of person who eats all day long, just total up everything you eat, and

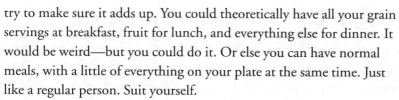

try to make sure it adds up. You could theoretically have all your grain servings at breakfast, fruit for lunch, and everything else for dinner. It would be weird—but you could do it. Or else you can have normal meals, with a little of everything on your plate at the same time. Just like a regular person. Suit yourself.

This food guide applies to a regular vegetarian diet that includes eggs and dairy products. Vegans (vegetarians who eat no animal foods whatever) should do a little *extra* homework to be sure they're eating a healthful diet. A doctor or school nutritionist will be able to give you the information you need.

Finally, an active person (who plays sports, dances, runs around like a maniac, etc.) will need to eat more of everything than a couch-potato type of individual. Do you fall somewhere in between? Eat what feels right for *you*.

Grain products (5 to 12 servings per day)

- Bread (absolutely any kind)
- Tortillas
- Crackers
- Cookies, muffins, and cakey things
- Pasta
- Rice, couscous, or bulgur wheat
- Barley, oats, cornmeal
- Cereals—all kinds, hot or cold

Vegetables and fruit (5 to 10 servings per day)

All fresh, frozen, canned, and dried fruits and vegetables, plus things like:
- Spaghetti sauce or salsa
- Raisins, dates, and other dried fruits
- Orange and other fruit juices
- Pickles and relishes

Milk products and alternatives (3 to 4 servings per day)

- Milk
- Cheese
- Yogurt or sour cream
- Cream cheese
- Processed cheese spread
- Soy milk

Meat alternatives (2 to 3 servings per day)

- Eggs
- Beans, peas, lentils
- Pretend meat (veggie burgers, veggie dogs, veggie nuggets)
- Tofu and tempeh
- Nuts and seeds (peanuts, almonds, walnuts, sunflower seeds, pumpkin seeds)

Vaguely Chinese Stir-Fry

The secret to a stir-fry is to have every single thing prepared before you start cooking so that you're not madly slicing or measuring in mid-fry. The preparation takes a while, but the actual cooking is done in no time.

1	bunch broccoli, florets cut off and into small pieces, stems sliced
1	green or red pepper, cut into 1-inch (2-cm) squares
4	green onions, halved lengthwise and cut into 1-inch (2 cm) pieces
2	squares tofu, frozen, thawed, and cut into ½ inch (1 cm) cubes
½ cup (125 mL)	vegetable broth or (if you prefer) chicken broth
3 tbsp (45 mL)	soy sauce
1 tbsp (15 mL)	cornstarch
1 tbsp (15 mL)	dry sherry (if you have it)
1 tsp (5 mL)	sesame oil
2	cloves garlic, squished
3 tbsp (45 mL)	vegetable oil
¼ cup (50 mL)	cashew nuts or peanuts (cashews really are better)

Arrange all the cut-up vegetables on a large plate, keeping each one in a separate pile. Cut up the tofu, and have it ready. In a small bowl, stir together ¼ cup (50 mL) of the broth, the soy sauce, cornstarch, sherry, and sesame oil, and set it aside. Have the garlic squished, and the cashews measured. OK, *now* you're ready to start cooking.

Pour about half of the vegetable oil into a wok or large skillet, and heat it over high heat. Toss in the tofu pieces, and stir-fry until very lightly browned. Scoop tofu out onto a plate, and set aside.

Add the rest of the vegetable oil to the wok or skillet, and let it get hot. Throw in the squished garlic, and stir-fry for 10 seconds, then right away add the broccoli and pepper. Stir-fry for 1 or 2 minutes. Add the onions, stir, and add the remaining ¼ cup (50 mL) of broth.

Bored?

Just when you think there's nothing fun left to do in the whole world, when you're feeling overwhelmed by responsibility, when you're just hanging aimlessly around the kitchen, try this. Dump some cornstarch (oh, about a cupful will do) into a bowl. Add water, a bit at a time, and stir. At first it will be a clumpy mixture but then, as you add drops of water, it begins to loosen up. Suddenly it's a liquid. No, it's a solid. No—*what the heck is this stuff, anyway?* Pick some up with your hand and let it ooze through your fingers. Squeeze it into a ball and it's hard again. Isn't life cool?

Slam a cover on the pan and let the vegetables steam for about 2 minutes, until the broccoli is lightly cooked. Finally, throw the tofu back into the pan, give it a good stir, and pour in the soy-sauce mixture, stirring constantly. The sauce will thicken and become glossy. Sprinkle the cashews or peanuts over the top, and serve immediately, with hot cooked rice or noodles.

Makes 3 or 4 servings.

Tofu (oh, come on, just try it)

Look, it's not made from seaweed or fish livers or anything weird like that. Tofu is a nice, wholesome food, made from perfectly harmless soybeans. It's packed with protein, low in fat, and cheap, cheap, cheap. It doesn't taste like anything on its own but absorbs the flavor of whatever it hangs out with. Try it a few different ways to see what you like.

Bake it! Buy extra-firm tofu, cut it into sticks or slabs, douse it with barbecue sauce, and bake until sizzling. Or dip extra-firm tofu fingers in beaten egg and bread crumbs and bake at 375° F (190° C) on an oiled cookie sheet until crisp (great with ketchup).

Stir-fry it! Marinate ½-inch (1 cm) cubes of regular tofu in soy sauce before stir-frying with veggies. It's *amazing* stir-fried with eggplant and hot chili sauce.

Freeze it! Throw a couple of squares of tofu into the freezer and let them freeze solid. Then thaw them out. The texture changes completely once it's been frozen. You can crumble it up (as a substitute for hamburger), or slice it into slivers to throw into a stir-fry.

Go naked! The tofu, that is. Just float a few cubes in your soup, or toss some with your salad. (Generally recommended for committed tofu converts only.)

Potato Paprikash

Who says you can't have potatoes for a main dish? Add a salad and you've got yourself a two-course dinner.

¼ cup (50 mL)	vegetable oil
3	onions, chopped
6	large potatoes, sliced ¼-inch (0.5 cm) thick
1 tbsp (15 mL)	paprika
½ tsp (2 mL)	salt
1 tsp (5 mL)	pepper
1 tsp (5 mL)	dried marjoram (if you have it)

Heat the oil in a large skillet. Add the onions and sauté for about 5 minutes, until softened. Add the potatoes and stir them around a little, then sprinkle with the paprika, salt, pepper, and marjoram. Cook for 2 minutes, then pour in enough water to *almost* (but not quite) cover the potatoes. Slam the lid on the pan, lower the heat to a simmer, and cook for 15 to 20 minutes, until the potatoes are tender when poked with a fork.

Makes 2 servings as a main dish, maybe 4 as a side dish.

Non-vegetarian alternative:

Add 6 hot dogs, cut into 1-inch (2 cm) pieces, to the pan with the onions. This turns the dish into *Hot Dog* Potato Paprikash—the humble hot dog's way to immortality.

Stuffed Baked Potatoes

Stash a couple of these in the fridge, wrapped in foil, for a very excellent dinner or midnight snack.

4	large potatoes
½ cup (125 mL)	cottage cheese
¼ cup (50 mL)	grated cheddar cheese
¼ cup (50 mL)	butter
½ tsp (2 mL)	salt
	pepper to taste

Preheat the oven to 400° F (200° C).

Scrub the potatoes, poke a few fork holes into each, then bake them at 400° F (200° C) until *really* done—about an hour. If you have a microwave, arrange the 4 potatoes in an X formation on a paper towel, and zap on high for 12 to 15 minutes (depending on your oven and the size of the potatoes). Flip the potatoes end to end and over about halfway through the baking time to make sure they cook evenly.

Cut a lengthwise slice from the top of each potato and carefully scoop out the insides. Mash them in a bowl with the cottage cheese, the cheddar cheese, the butter, the salt, and the pepper.

Spoon the mixture back into the shells, mounding the filling on top. You can leave them *au naturel*, or sprinkle them with a little paprika to be extra cheerful. Place on a baking sheet, if you'll be baking them right away, or wrap in foil, and put in the fridge for future consumption.

About 15 minutes before you'll want to eat, put the potatoes back into a 400° F (200° C) oven and bake until heated through, and very lightly browned.

Serves 4 as a side dish, fewer as a main course.

Potato and Pea Curry

A jar of chutney, some sliced cucumbers, a bowl of yogurt—your karma will thank you.

6	medium potatoes
¼ cup (50 mL)	vegetable oil
1 tsp (5 mL)	whole mustard seeds
2	onions, chopped
1 tbsp (15 mL)	curry powder
1 cup (250 mL)	frozen peas
1 tsp (5 mL)	salt
1 cup (250 mL)	water
¼ cup (50 mL)	chopped cilantro (also called coriander) (if you have it) or fresh parsley
¼ tsp (1 mL)	cayenne pepper (or as much as you like)

Cook the potatoes in boiling water until tender, but still a little firm in the middle. Drain, let cool for a couple of minutes, then peel them (they should practically peel themselves) and cut into ½-inch (1 cm) cubes.

In a large skillet, heat the oil over medium heat, and add the mustard seeds. Enjoy the show, as they crackle and pop in the pan, then add the onions. Cook, stirring, over medium heat, for 5 to 7 minutes, until golden. Add the curry powder, stir for a couple of minutes, and then add the potatoes, peas, salt, and water. Reduce the heat to low, cover the skillet, and cook for about 5 minutes. Add the cilantro and cayenne, cook for another 10 minutes, adding a bit more water, if it gets too dry.

Makes 2 or 3 servings.

Eggplant Parmigiana

Every vegetarian needs a few recipes that can be hauled out when carnivores (your parents?) come to dinner. This is a good one. No one will care that there's no meat.

½ cup (125 mL)	vegetable oil
2	eggs
½ cup (125 mL)	milk
2 cups (500 mL)	dry bread crumbs
½ tsp (2 mL)	oregano
½ tsp (2 mL)	salt
¼ tsp (1 mL)	pepper
2	medium eggplants
4 cups (1 L)	spaghetti sauce, homemade or canned, any kind
½ cup (125 mL)	grated Parmesan cheese
3 cups (750 mL)	grated mozzarella cheese

Preheat the broiler element of your oven. Brush a baking sheet with just enough of the vegetable oil to coat it lightly.

In a small dish, beat the eggs with the milk. In another dish, combine the bread crumbs, oregano, salt, and pepper.

Peel the eggplants, trim off the ends, and slice them into ¼-inch (0.5 cm) rounds. Dip the eggplant slices first into the egg mixture, then into the bread crumbs, turning to coat both sides. Arrange a few slices on the oiled baking sheet (don't let them overlap) and broil for about 3 to 4 minutes, then flip the slices over and broil for another 3 to 4 minutes. The eggplant should be lightly browned on both sides, and tender when you poke a fork in it. Remove the slices from the baking sheet, brush on a bit more oil, and repeat until you've done all the eggplant slices. You may not need to use all the entire ½ cup (125 mL) of the oil.

Turn off the broiler and set the oven to 350° F (180° C).

Spread ½ cup (125 mL) of the spaghetti sauce on the bottom of a 9 × 13-inch (22 × 33 cm) baking dish (just a thin layer). On this, arrange a layer of eggplant slices, cutting them, if necessary, to cover the bottom. Spread with 1 cup (250 mL) of spaghetti sauce, a sprinkle of Parmesan cheese, and 1 cup (250 mL) of mozzarella cheese. Repeat— another layer of eggplant slices, another cup of spaghetti sauce, a sprinkle of Parmesan, and a cup of mozzarella. And finally, all the rest of the eggplant slices, all the rest of the spaghetti sauce, and all the rest of the Parmesan cheese. Hang on to the mozzarella—you'll need it later.

Bake at 350° F (180° C) for 30 minutes. Sprinkle on all of that mozzarella cheese you were saving, and bake for another 15 minutes, until bubbling and the cheese is melted.

Makes 6 to 8 servings.

Welsh Rabbit

You will, no doubt, be relieved to learn that no actual rabbits are used in this recipe.

2 tbsp (30 mL)	**butter**
½ cup (125 mL)	**beer (leftover flat beer is fine)**
1	**egg**
2 tsp (10 mL)	**mustard**
1 tsp (5 mL)	**Worcestershire sauce**
3 cups (750 mL)	**grated sharp cheddar cheese**
2	**tomatoes, sliced**
some	**toasted English muffins, or toasted French bread, or toasted anything**

In a small saucepan, melt the butter. Whisk together the beer, egg, mustard, and Worcestershire sauce, and add to the butter along with the cheese. Cook this mixture, stirring, over very low heat until smooth and thickened, about 8 minutes.

On individual plates, lay slices of tomato over the toasted English muffins, or whatever you have that's toasted, and pour the cheese sauce over all.

Makes 3 or 4 servings.

How to Cook Dried Beans

Sure, you can buy your kidney beans in a can. And, there's nothing wrong with them. But for sheer down-and-dirty cheapness, nothing beats a bag of good old dried beans. Cooking them doesn't even take that long.

Measure your beans (any kind) into a saucepan. Look them over carefully, and remove all the little alien bits that you find—pebbles, bits of dirt, weirdly deformed beans. Cover them with cold water, swish them around a bit with your hand, and pour the water off. Do it again, just to be sure the beans are well washed—you never know where they've been.

Next you'll have to soak them. If you've planned ahead, you can just cover the beans with plenty of cold water and let them sit at room temperature overnight. Or if you *didn't* plan ahead, you can quick-soak them. Add enough fresh, cold water to the pan to cover the beans by at least 1½ to 2 inches (4 to 5 cm). Place on the stove, cover, and bring to a boil over high heat. Let boil for 2 minutes, then turn off the heat and let the beans sit for 1 hour.

To cook, pour off the soaking water, and add enough cold water to cover the beans by about 1 inch (2.5 cm). You might also add a couple of whole cloves of garlic, and a whole peeled onion for extra flavor. Don't add salt—it toughens the beans. Cover the pot, bring to a boil over medium heat, and cook until the beans are soft. Depending on the type of bean, and how fresh it is, this could take anywhere from 30 minutes to 2 hours. Don't let the water boil away.

Drain the beans, salt them to taste, and use them in whatever way you'd use canned ones. If you have to keep them for a while before using, leave your cooked beans in their liquid.

Bean and Vegetable Stew

*It's a dark and stormy night. Wouldn't a nice warm bowl of this
stew be just perfect?*

1	medium eggplant, cut into 1-inch (2 cm) cubes
¼ cup (50 mL)	olive or vegetable oil
4	cloves garlic, squished
2	medium onions, cut into 1-inch (2 cm) chunks
1	medium zucchini, cut into 1-inch (2 cm) chunks
2	peppers—any color—cut into 1-inch (2 cm) squares
4	medium potatoes, peeled and cut into 1-inch (2 cm) cubes
2 cups (500 mL)	fresh mushrooms, cut into quarters
1 28-oz (796 mL)	can tomatoes, smashed up a bit
½ cup (125 mL)	vegetable (or chicken) broth
1 5½-oz (156 mL)	can tomato paste
1 19-oz (540 mL)	can beans—red or white kidney, romano, black, whatever

Place the cubed eggplant into a colander set over a bowl and toss with
1 tsp (5 mL) salt. Let it sit for 1 hour to allow the liquid to drip out,
then rinse under running water, and pat the cubes dry with paper towel.
(This removes some of the excess liquid from the eggplant.) Proceed.

Preheat the oven to 375° F (190° C).

In a large skillet, heat half of the oil over medium heat until hot.
Add the eggplant and garlic, and sauté for 5 to 8 minutes, until golden.
Remove and place in a very large casserole or roasting pan. Add the rest
of oil to the pan, and sauté the onions, zucchini, peppers, potatoes, and
mushrooms just until the onions soften, about 5 minutes. Add to the
casserole with the eggplant. Add the tomatoes, broth, tomato paste, and
beans, and mix well to combine everything. Cover with a lid (if you
have one) or foil, and bake at 375° F (190° C) for 1 hour. Remove the
lid for the last 15 minutes to allow the top to brown slightly.

Serve this with something that will soak up the sauce—like rice, or
couscous, or pasta.

Makes 8 servings.

Meatless Chili

Years ago, when great herds of wild eggplants roamed the wide prairies, clever cooks invented this chili to make use of the seemingly endless supply.

1	large eggplant, peeled and cut into 1/2-inch (1 cm) cubes
1 tbsp (15 mL)	salt
¼ cup (50 mL)	oil
2	onions, chopped
2	medium zucchini, cut in ½-inch (1 cm) cubes
2	red or green peppers (or one of each), chopped
4	cloves garlic, squished
1 28-oz (796 mL)	can tomatoes, broken up
3 tbsp (45 mL)	chili powder
1 tbsp (15 mL)	ground cumin
1 tbsp (15 mL)	oregano
1 tsp (5 mL)	pepper
½ tsp (2 mL)	hot pepper flakes (or more, or less)
½ tsp (2 mL)	salt
1 19-oz (540 mL)	can red kidney or pinto beans
1½ cups (375 mL)	frozen or canned corn niblets

Place the eggplant cubes in a colander or strainer set over a bowl, and sprinkle with the 1 tbsp (15 mL) of salt to draw out the excess water from the eggplant. Let it drain for about an hour, then pat it dry with paper towel. If you're in a big hurry, you can skip this step.

Heat the oil in a large, heavy pot and cook the onions, zucchini, peppers, and garlic over medium heat for about 5 minutes, until softened. Add the eggplant, and cook for another 5 or 10 minutes, until everything is tender. Add the tomatoes and all their juice, the chili powder, cumin, oregano, pepper, hot pepper flakes, and salt and bring to a boil. Cook over low heat for about 30 minutes, stirring once in a while.

Now dump in the beans and the corn, and cook for another 15 minutes. Taste, and adjust the seasoning if necessary.

Serve hot, over rice, with a glop of sour cream, a sprinkle of grated cheese, some chopped jalapeño peppers, *whatever*.

Makes about 8 servings.

Couscous with Vegetables

Fast and delicious, couscous goes with anything you care to spoon onto it, and will make you look like a really adventurous cook. Just smile mysteriously and never admit it was so easy.

½ cup (125 mL)	vegetable oil
1	onion, chopped
2	cloves garlic, squished
1½ cups (375 mL)	vegetable (or chicken) broth
1 cup (250 mL)	peeled and cubed raw butternut or other hard-shelled squash
1 cup (250 mL)	sliced carrots
½ tsp (2 mL)	ground ginger
½ tsp (2 mL)	ground cumin
¼ tsp (1 mL)	hot pepper flakes (or more, or less, or none)
½ tsp (2 mL)	salt
½ tsp (2 mL)	pepper
1	medium zucchini, cut into chunks
1 19-oz (540 mL)	can chick peas, drained
1	medium tomato, cut into chunks
¼ cup (50 mL)	raisins (sort of optional)
¼ cup (50 mL)	chopped fresh parsley
¾ cup (175 mL)	couscous
¾ cup (175 mL)	boiling water

In a large skillet, heat the oil over medium heat, add the onion and garlic, and sauté for about 2 minutes, until softened. Pour in the vegetable broth, the squash, carrots, the ginger, cumin, hot pepper flakes, salt, and pepper. Cover, bring to a boil, and simmer for 5 to 10 minutes, until the vegetables are just tender. Add the zucchini, chick peas, and tomato and cook another 2 minutes. Stir in the raisins and parsley.

While the vegetable concoction is cooking, make the couscous. In a small bowl, stir the boiling water into the dry couscous, cover it (with a plate or lid), and let stand for 5 minutes. The water will be absorbed into the couscous, and the grains will be separate, but fluff them up by stirring with a fork.

Spoon some couscous onto each plate, top with some of the vegetable mixture, and serve.

Makes 3 or 4 servings.

Veggie Burgers

Oh, stop whining. Here's something to throw on the barbecue when all your friends are eating hamburgers. In fact, you'd better make extra—your carnivorous pals will be begging for a taste.

1½ cups (375 mL)	chopped red and/or green peppers
2 tbsp (30 mL)	vegetable oil
1½ cups (375 mL)	grated raw carrots (about 3 carrots)
2 cups (500 mL)	cleaned and chopped raw spinach, tightly packed
3	potatoes, boiled and mashed (about 2 cups/500 mL)
1	large onion, grated
3	eggs, beaten
1 tsp (5 mL)	salt
	pepper to taste
1 cup (250 mL)	bread crumbs

Sauté the chopped peppers in the oil until soft, about 10 to 15 minutes. Dump them into a large bowl, add all the other ingredients, mix very well, and let the mixture stand, refrigerated, for at least an hour (or overnight).

By hand, form this mixture into burgers, flattening them slightly.

To grill your veggie burgers, brush them lightly on both sides with a little vegetable oil, and cook on the barbecue over low heat for about 10 minutes per side. To make sure they cook right through, turn them over a couple of times as they cook.

Or, instead, you can fry these babies. Heat some vegetable oil in a large skillet and cook the veggie burgers over medium heat until golden brown on both sides.

Makes about 10 veggie burgers.

Mushrooms on Toast

Does it seem weird to just eat mushrooms for dinner? Add some soup and a salad, and you'll feel normal.

2 tbsp (30 mL)	**butter**
2 tbsp (30 mL)	**olive oil**
1	**onion, finely chopped**
2	**cloves garlic, squished**
1 lb (500 g)	**fresh mushrooms, sliced**
	juice of 1 lemon
¼ cup (50 mL)	**chopped parsley**
	salt and pepper
some	**toasted French or other nice bread**

In a medium skillet, melt the butter with the olive oil over medium heat. Sauté the onion and garlic until softened, about 5 minutes. Add the mushrooms and cook over fairly high heat, until they begin to soften and release their juices. Add the lemon juice to the pan, sprinkle with the parsley, and cook for another 1 or 2 minutes. Season with salt and pepper, and spoon over toasted French bread.

Makes 2 servings.

Vegetarian Cowboy Beans

After riding the range all day—rounding up those herds of wild egg-plants—vegetarian cowboys like to sit around the old campfire with a heaping plateful of these beans and tell some lies.

1 lb (500 g)	white pea or navy beans
4 cups (1 L)	water
2	medium onions, chopped
1 tbsp (15 mL)	vinegar
1 tbsp (15 mL)	prepared mustard
¼ cup (50 mL)	brown sugar
¼ cup (50 mL)	molasses
½ cup (125 mL)	ketchup
2 tbsp (30 mL)	vegetable oil
1 tsp (5 mL)	salt
2	tomatoes, thickly sliced

Put the dry beans into a large pot and pick over them carefully, removing any bits that don't look like a bean (pebbles, bits of dirt, that sort of thing). Then rinse them well, changing the water several times to wash off the dirt. Cover the beans with plenty of fresh water—about 1 or 2 inches (2.5 cm) over the beans—and let them soak for at least 12 hours, or overnight.

Drain the beans thoroughly—they should have nearly doubled in size—and discard the soaking water. Pour in the 4 cups (1 L) of fresh water, heat to boiling, cover, and simmer for 30 minutes.

Once again, drain the beans, reserving the cooking liquid. Place the chopped onions into the bottom of an ovenproof pot with a lid (a Dutch oven or medium-size casserole is good), and add the beans. In a small bowl, mix together the vinegar, mustard, sugar, molasses, ketchup, oil, and salt. Pour this over the beans, then pour in enough of the reserved cooking liquid so it just covers the beans, adding a bit more water if necessary. Arrange the tomato slices over the top, cover with the lid, and bake at 250° F (120° C) for 7 hours. Really. Seven.

About halfway through the cooking time, lift the lid, and give the pot a stir. Replace the cover, and continue baking until the 7 hours are up, adding a little additional liquid to keep the beans just covered. You can remove the cover for the last hour of baking to let them brown a bit.

Now, go sit around the fire, eat your beans, and tell some lies. It's been a long day on the range.

Makes 8 servings.

Bean Burritos

Who says you don't have time to make dinner? Here. This will take two minutes.

Burrito supplies

>Flour tortillas (*not* optional)
>Refried beans, homemade or canned, heated
> in a microwave or skillet
>Shredded cheddar or Monterey Jack cheese
>Salsa (hot or mild)
>Sour cream
>Diced tomatoes
>Shredded lettuce
>Chopped onion
>Chopped jalapeño peppers

Burrito construction:

Drop a large blob of warm refried beans onto the middle of your tortilla. Top the beans with any or all of the above ingredients, in whatever order or amount that seems logical.

Now, fold the bottom of the tortilla up so that it partly covers the beans (etc.). Next, fold one side in toward the middle, then fold in the other side. Leave the top open. There. Done.

Pick it up and eat. Or take it with you. Bye.

Baking Up a Storm

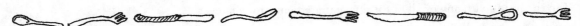

It's not fair. Maybe you cook a world-class chicken. Or a mean meat loaf. Or a spectacular spaghetti. Does anyone notice? Does anyone care? But make a batch of chocolate chip cookies and everyone goes crazy. Learn to bake. It's your only hope.

Basic Homemade Muffins

Even a bad homemade muffin, freshly baked and still warm, is much better than anything you can buy anywhere. Try not to eat them all yourself.

1¾ cup (425 mL)	flour
¼ cup (50 mL)	sugar
2½ tsp (12 mL)	baking powder
1	egg, beaten
¾ cup (175 mL)	milk
⅓ cup (75 mL)	vegetable oil
	Optional ingredients: 1 cup (250 mL) blueberries or cranberries (washed), or ¾ cup (175 mL) raisins, chopped nuts, or chocolate chips

Preheat the oven to 400° F (200° C).

Measure the flour, sugar, and baking powder into a medium bowl. In a small bowl, whisk together the egg, milk, and oil, and add all at once to the flour mixture. Stir just until the flour is completely moistened, but don't overmix—a few lumps are OK. Gently stir in any optional ingredients, if you're using them.

Spoon batter into a well-greased or paper-lined muffin pan, filling the cups almost to the top. Bake at 400° F (200° C) for 20 to 25 minutes, until a toothpick poked into the middle of a muffin comes out clean.

Makes about 9 or 10 muffins.

Beautiful Bran Muffins

Regular bran (as opposed to bran flakes or bran cereal) is dirt cheap. A bag of it will last you forever, produce tons of muffins, and is good for doctoring a horse's sore leg, besides. Hey, you never know.

½ cup (125 mL)	vegetable oil
¾ cup (175 mL)	brown sugar
1	egg
1 cup (250 mL)	flour
1 tsp (5 mL)	baking soda
1 cup (250 mL)	buttermilk, yogurt, or soured milk (see page 42)
1½ cups (375 mL)	bran (*not* bran flakes)
½ cup (125 mL)	raisins (optional, for raisin lovers)

Preheat the oven to 375° F (190° C).

In a large bowl, whisk together the vegetable oil, brown sugar, and egg until smooth. In a small bowl, combine the flour with the baking soda. Add the flour mixture to the egg mixture in 2 or 3 portions, alternating with the buttermilk (or yogurt, or soured milk), stirring just until everything is evenly moistened. Stir in the bran and the raisins, if you're using them.

Spoon batter into a muffin pan that's been well greased or one with paper muffin cups fitted inside, filling the cups almost to the top. Bake at 375° F (190° C) for 20 to 25 minutes, until a toothpick poked into the middle of a muffin comes out clean.

Makes 10 to 12 muffins.

Banana Bread

You know those bananas you forgot to eat? The black ones?
Give them another chance—make some banana bread.

1¼ cups (300 mL)	flour
1 cup (250 mL)	sugar
1 tsp (5 mL)	baking soda
½ cup (125 mL)	butter, margarine, or vegetable oil
2	very ripe bananas
2	eggs

Preheat oven to 350°F (180°C).

In a large bowl, mix together the flour, sugar, and baking soda.

Put all the rest of the ingredients into the blender—the butter (or margarine or oil), the bananas, and the eggs—and let 'er rip! Blend this until smooth.

Pour the blended banana mixture into the flour mixture, and stir until thoroughly combined.

Spoon the batter into a well-greased loaf pan, and bake at 350° F (180° C) for about 1 hour. If you want, you can bake this in muffin pans instead. Grease the cups (or use paper cups), fill them almost to the top, and bake at 350° F (180° C) for about 30 minutes.

Makes 1 loaf or about 10 muffins.

Cornbread

Absolutely nothing goes better with a pot of chili than fresh cornbread.

1½ cups (375 mL)	white flour
1 cup (250 mL)	yellow cornmeal
¼ cup (50 mL)	sugar
2 tbsp (30 mL)	baking powder
½ tsp (2 mL)	salt
¼ cup (50 mL)	vegetable oil
1	egg
1⅓ cups (325 mL)	milk

First, grease an 8-inch (20 cm) square baking pan and preheat the oven to 350° F (180° C).

In a large bowl, stir together the flour, the cornmeal, the sugar, the baking powder, and the salt. In a smaller bowl, beat together the oil, the egg, and the milk. Now pour the milk mixture into the flour mixture, and stir together with a wooden spoon, until pretty well combined. A few lumps are OK, so don't beat it to death.

Pour batter into the baking pan, spreading so that the top is even. Bake for about 15 minutes, or until a toothpick poked into the middle comes out clean.

Let cool for just a couple of minutes before cutting into squares.

Makes about 9 big hunks of cornbread, or more smaller ones.

Irish Soda Bread

For this (extremely easy) bread, you'll have to buy a carton of buttermilk—but don't let that scare you. You'll use half of it to make the bread, and then you can either drink the rest plain (it's tart, and yogurty-tasting), whip up an amazing fruit milkshake, make some real buttermilk pancakes, or bake a batch of muffins. Or you can just make another loaf of bread.

3½ to 4 cups **(800 to 900 mL)**	**white flour**
1 cup (250 mL)	**raisins (or less)**
¼ cup (50 mL)	**caraway seeds (or less, or none)**
1½ tbsp (20 mL)	**baking powder**
1 tsp (5 mL)	**salt**
2 cups (500 mL)	**buttermilk**
1	**egg**
2 tbsp (30 mL)	**honey**
¼ tsp (1 mL)	**baking soda**

Preheat the oven to 375° F (190° C).

In a *large* bowl, combine the 3½ cups (800 mL) of the flour, the raisins, caraway seeds, baking powder, and salt. Stir well to mix ingredients thoroughly.

In a medium bowl, stir together the buttermilk, egg, honey, and baking soda. Immediately *(really immediately)* pour this mixture into the flour mixture, and stir well until everything is blended. Although this dough doesn't really have to be kneaded, it's really easier to mix the gucky stuff by hand, rather than try to wrestle it with a spoon. Just keep the dough in the bowl—it's pretty soft. If it's much too soft to easily form into a loaf, add a little more flour until you can handle it.

Squash the dough into a well-greased loaf pan, and bake at 375° F (190° C) for 1 hour and 15 minutes, or until the loaf is nicely browned, and a toothpick poked into the middle of it comes out clean.

It's not true that warm bread will give you a stomach ache—go ahead, have a slice.

 # Absolutely Basic Yeast Dough

Yeast. Does the word send shivers down your spine? Do you freeze up when you imagine using such a thing? Relax. We'll start with something very simple. This dough is the basis for focaccia bread, pizza crust, and garlic breadsticks. It's fun to do, unbelievably easy, and everyone will think you're a genius. How can you lose?

1 cup (250 mL)	warm *(not hot)* water
1 envelope (15 mL)	active dry yeast
3½ cups (875 mL)	white flour *(approximately)*
1 tbsp (15 mL)	vegetable or olive oil
1 tsp (5 mL)	salt

Pour the warm water into a large bowl, and sprinkle in the dry yeast. Give it a stir, then wait 5 minutes. The yeast, awakened from dormancy, comes to life! (AAAAGH!!!) It bubbles and goes all weird in the bowl. Or at least it should. If that doesn't happen, wait another 5 minutes. If *still* nothing happens, throw the mixture out and start over with a fresh package of yeast—the poor thing may have been too old.

Add 1 cup (250 mL) of the flour, the oil, and the salt to the yeast mixture, and stir until smooth. Add the rest of the flour, 1 cup (250 mL) at a time, until the dough becomes too stiff to stir easily. When this happens, sprinkle about ½ cup (125 mL) of flour out onto a board (or the table), turn the dough out of the bowl, and begin kneading. This is the fun part. Squash the dough down with the heel of your hand, while turning and folding, over and over and over again for about 10 minutes. If the dough sticks to the board, sprinkle it with a little more flour. How do you know when it's ready? Pinch the dough gently between your fingers—when it feels like your earlobe, it's done. It should be smooth, stretchy, and no longer sticky on the surface.

Place the dough in a large oiled bowl, turn it over so that all the surfaces are greased, and place the bowl on the top shelf of your oven. *DO NOT TURN THE OVEN ON!* Put a large pot of very hot water on the bottom of the oven, close the door, and let the dough rise in this warm, moist place for about 1½ hours, until almost double in volume.

Remove the dough from the oven, admire it for a minute, then make a fist and punch the dough right in the gizzard to deflate it. Turn it out of the bowl, knead it a few times, and set it aside while you pre-pare to *create something*.

For further details see the recipes for focaccia bread (page 187), pizza (page 182), or garlic breadsticks (page 180).

See—that wasn't so hard, was it?

Antidepressant Brownies

You flunked the geography test. You lost your favorite sweater. You had a fight with your best friend. It's raining. You need some brownies.

¾ cup (175 mL)	unsweetened cocoa powder
½ tsp (2 mL)	baking soda
⅔ cup (150 mL)	oil
½ cup (125 mL)	boiling water
2 cups (500 mL)	sugar
2	eggs
1⅓ cup (325 mL)	flour
1 tsp (5 mL)	vanilla
1 cup (250 mL)	coarsely chopped walnuts or pecans (optional, for severe depression)

Preheat the oven to 350° F (180° C).

Grease a 9 × 13-inch (22 × 33 cm) baking pan.

In a large bowl, stir together the cocoa and baking soda. Blend in ⅓ cup (75 mL) of the oil, and mix until smooth. Pour in the boiling water, stirring until the mixture thickens—for complex scientific reasons it *will* thicken. Now stir in the rest of the oil, the sugar, and the eggs. Mix until smooth.

Add the flour and the vanilla. Blend completely—there should be no lumps. Now mix in the nuts (if you're using them), and pour into the greased baking pan. Spread the batter evenly to avoid crispy edges—not a good thing in a brownie.

Bake at 350°F (180° C) for 35 to 40 minutes, until just set in the mid-dle. Don't overcook brownies—they are always better when slightly soggy.

Let cool and cut into squares. But you can't wait that long, can you? Oh, all right, eat them hot—despite what your mom told you, warm brownies won't make you sick.

Makes about 20 brownies.

 # Classic Chocolate Chip Cookies

Nothing on this planet comes even remotely close to the wonderfulness of a homemade chocolate chip cookie. Nothing. Why don't you make a batch right now? You know you want to.

1 cup (250 mL)	butter
¾ cup (175 mL)	white sugar
¾ cup (175 mL)	brown sugar
2	eggs
1 tsp (5 mL)	vanilla
2¼ cups (550 mL)	flour
1 tsp (5 mL)	baking soda
¼ tsp (1 mL)	salt (optional)
2 cups (500 mL)	chocolate chips
1 cup (250 mL)	chopped walnuts or pecans (optional)

Preheat the oven to 375° F (190° C).

In a large bowl, with an electric mixer, or in a food processor (if you have one), beat together the butter with the white and brown sugars, eggs, and vanilla until nice and fluffy.

In a smaller bowl, combine the flour with the baking soda (and the salt), and then add to the creamed mixture, beating until smooth and blended. Stir in the chocolate chips by hand. At this point, certain persons might add nuts.

Drop the dough by spoonfuls onto an ungreased cookie sheet about 2 inches (5 cm) apart, and bake at 375° F (190° C) for 10 to 12 minutes, or until the edges are just browned, but the cookies are still soft in the middle. Carefully remove the cookies to a rack and try not to eat them all before they are cool.

Makes 6 to 8 dozen, depending on the size and how much dough you ate.

Official Peanut Butter Cookies

Remember when you were little and your mom used to wait for you with a plate of peanut butter cookies and a glass of milk? No? Did anyone's mom ever do that? I guess you'll just have to make them for yourself.

½ cup (125 mL)	butter or margarine
½ cup (125 mL)	peanut butter
½ cup (125 mL)	white sugar
½ cup (125 mL)	brown sugar
1	egg
1¼ (300 mL)	cup flour (white or whole wheat)
½ tsp (2 mL)	baking powder
½ tsp (2 mL)	baking soda
½ cup (125 mL)	chocolate chips (optional, but very good)

Line a cookie sheet (or two) with aluminum foil, and preheat the oven to 375° F (190° C).

In a large bowl, with an electric mixer, beat together the butter, peanut butter, white and brown sugars, and the egg until smooth and creamy. Add the flour, baking powder, and baking soda, and mix until smooth.

By hand, roll the dough into 1-inch (2 cm) balls and place them 2 inches (5 cm) apart on the foil-lined cookie sheet. Now, here's the thing: *flatten each ball in a criss-cross pattern with a fork.* This *crucial* step is what makes them *official* peanut butter cookies. Do not, under any circumstances, forget to do this. And finally, if you haven't eaten all the chocolate chips, press 3 or 4 into each cookie.

Bake at 375° F (190° C) for 10 to 12 minutes, until golden brown. The cookies will still be a bit soft, but they'll harden when they cool.

Makes 3½ dozen.

 # No-Nonsense Oatmeal Cookies

Sort of plain, crisp, nothing weird about them at all. The perfect cookie for when you're feeling especially unadventurous.

1 cup (250 mL)	**flour (white or whole wheat)**
½ tsp (2 mL)	**baking powder**
½ tsp (2 mL)	**baking soda**
½ cup (125 mL)	**butter or margarine**
½ cup (125 mL)	**white sugar**
½ cup (125 mL)	**brown sugar**
1	**egg**
1 tsp (5 mL)	**vanilla extract**
½ cup (125 mL)	**rolled oats (not instant)**
1 cup (250 mL)	**finely shredded coconut**

Line a cookie sheet (or 2) with aluminum foil, and preheat the oven to 375° F (190° C).

In a medium bowl, stir together the flour, baking powder, and baking soda. In another bowl, with an electric mixer, beat together the butter, the brown and white sugars, the egg, and the vanilla until light and fluffy. Stir the flour mixture into the butter mixture (gradually, a scoop at a time), and mix until smooth. Finally, stir in the oats and coconut.

Drop the batter by teaspoons onto the ungreased, foil-lined cookie sheet, leaving 1½ inches (4 cm) between blobs, to allow for spreading. Don't bother flattening them down—they'll flatten themselves. Bake at 375° F (190° C) for 10 to 12 minutes, until lightly browned on the edges.

Makes 4 dozen cookies.

Desserts

Oh, they'll be polite enough through dinner. But they're really all waiting for dessert. Don't disappoint them.

Me? Make a Pie? Are You Kidding?!?

No. Not kidding. Here—try it.

To make a pie crust, sprinkle a board and one ball of the dough with flour. Using a rolling pin, gently roll the dough out—first in one direction, then another, always working from the center of the ball outward. If it begins to stick to the board, sprinkle with some more flour. When it looks as if it's big enough, carefully fold the dough in half over on itself and lift it into your pie pan. Unfold it, and gently squish it down into the pan. Don't stretch it, or pull it, or tear it. Trim the edges and do something fancy and frilly to them by pinching all the way around. Did you get a hole in your pastry? Patch it with a bit of dough. No one will suspect.

An Actual Pie Made by You

See—it's not that hard.

1 recipe	Foolproof Multipurpose Pie Crust (page 159)
4 cups (1 L)	fruit (see sidebar)
2 tbsp (30 mL)	plain dry bread crumbs
½ to 1 cup	sugar
(125 mL to 250 mL)	
¼ cup (50 mL)	flour
½ tsp (2 mL)	cinnamon (optional, depending on the fruit)

Preheat the oven to 425° F (220° C).

Roll out 1 ball of pastry dough (half the recipe) on a well-floured surface, into a circle about 1 inch (2.5 cm) larger all around than the pie pan you'll be using. So, if you have a 9-inch (22 cm) pie pan, roll the dough out to about 11 inches (28 cm). The edges may be a bit rough—don't worry about it. Carefully fold the rolled dough in half, and lift it gently into the pie pan. Unfold, and fit it evenly into the pan without stretching it. There will be a bit of dough overhanging the edges. Using a sharp knife, cut this off even with the edge of the pan. Sprinkle the bread crumbs into the pie crust.

In a large bowl, mix together your prepared fruit with the sugar, flour, and cinnamon (if you're using it). Dump into the crust, mounding it up slightly in the middle.

Roll the rest of the pastry dough out (the other half of the recipe), again on a well-floured surface, into another circle about the same size as before. Fold the pastry in half, lift it carefully, and place it onto the filled pie crust. Unfold and let the edges hang over the sides. If there is more than about ½ inch (1 cm) overhanging dough, cut it off with a sharp knife or scissors. Now, very gently, tuck the edges of the top crust under the edges of the bottom crust in order to keep everything enclosed. With your fingers, firmly pinch the edges together to make a frilly-looking border. Cut 3 or 4 slits in the top of the crust for steam vents.

Bake at 425° F (220° C) for 45 to 50 minutes, or until the fruit is tender and bubbling.

Wow! Did you make that?

Fruit pie fillings:

Apple
Peel, core, and slice apples thinly.

Peach
Peel, pit, and slice peaches thinly. Add 1 tbsp (15 mL) cornstarch to the filling.

Rhubarb
Wash the rhubarb stalks, cut off the ends, and cut up into ½-inch (1 cm) pieces. Add 2 tbsp (30 mL) cornstarch to the filling. Try it half and half with strawberries.

Blueberry
Wash berries, and remove any little stemmy bits or leaves. Add 2 tbsp (30 mL) cornstarch to the filling.

Foolproof Multipurpose Pie Crust

This easy pastry dough can be used whenever you need a pie crust—for a dessert, or a quiche.

2 cups (500 mL)	flour
1 tsp (5 mL)	sugar
⅔ cup (150 mL)	solid vegetable shortening (not butter or margarine)
1	egg
1 tsp (5 mL)	vinegar
	cold water

Measure the flour and sugar into a bowl, and stir to mix. Cut the shortening up into chunks, and toss it into the bowl with the flour. Now, using a pastry blender (ask your mom) or two knives (one in each hand), chop the shortening into the flour until it looks all crumbly. The idea is to cut the shortening (the fat) up into teensy tiny bits, and mix it into the flour but don't blend it the way you'd mix cookie batter. The mixture should look something like uncooked oatmeal or bread crumbs.

Crack the egg into a measuring cup, add the vinegar, and scramble it up. Pour in enough cold water to equal *a scant* (that means *less than*) ½ cup (125 mL). Add the liquid to the flour mixture, and stir just until the dough can be formed into a ball. Don't overstir this.

Cut the dough in half and form each half into a flattish round. Refrigerate for at least 1 hour before using.

Use this pastry in any recipe that calls for a pie crust. If you don't need the second crust, wrap it tightly and freeze it to use some other time.

Makes enough dough for two single pie crusts—to make 1 double-crust pie or 2 shells.

There. A piece of cake—er, *pie*.

Bread Pudding

You know that old bread you were going to feed to the birds? Well, hang on just a second. Try this instead. The birds can wait.

4 cups (1 L)	bread cubes, any kind (slightly stale is fine, but *moldy* is not)
½ cup (125 mL)	raisins
4	eggs
3 cups (750 mL)	milk
½ tsp (2 mL)	cinnamon
¼ tsp (1 mL)	nutmeg
½ cup (125 mL)	sugar
1 tsp (5 mL)	vanilla

Place the bread cubes in a well-greased 9 × 13-inch (22 × 33 cm) baking dish. Sprinkle the raisins over the bread.

In a bowl, beat together the eggs, milk, cinnamon, nutmeg, sugar, and vanilla. Pour this mixture over the bread cubes, and leave them to soak, covered with plastic wrap, for several hours or overnight.

Bake at 325° F (160° C) for 35 to 40 minutes, until puffed and golden. Serve warm, with cream or ice cream, if you have it. Or just sprinkled with some icing sugar, if you don't.

Makes 6 to 8 servings.

Baked Apples

A nice, squishy baked apple will make you feel very virtuous. If you don't want to feel so virtuous, have some ice cream with it.

6	medium apples (Macintosh, Spy, Cortland or Idared are good apples for baking—just don't use Red Delicious)
½ cup (125 mL)	sugar
¼ tsp (1 mL)	cinnamon
2 tbsp (30 mL)	butter
1 cup (250 mL)	boiling water

Preheat the oven to 400° F (200° C).

Wash and core the apples, *not quite* all the way through to the bottom. Remove a strip of peel from around each apple, about ⅓ of the way down from the top (to prevent the apple from splitting when it bakes). Arrange the apples in a buttered baking dish, just large enough to hold them all—a pie pan, for example.

In a small bowl, combine the sugar and the cinnamon. Fill the cavity of each apple, almost to the top, with this mixture, then seal the top with a dab of butter.

Pour the boiling water into the dish around the apples, and bake at 400° F (200° C) for 40 to 45 minutes, basting them every 10 minutes or so with the liquid in the pan.

Let the apples cool before serving, and serve warm or cold, with ice cream or just plain with a spoonful of the baking liquid drizzled over top.

Makes 6 servings.

Self-Saucing Hot Fudge Pudding

This deadly dessert should be reserved for moments of deepest chocolate desperation. Beware—this is not for the timid.

1 cup (250 mL)	flour
1½ cups (375 mL)	sugar *(total amount)*
2 tsp (10 mL)	baking powder
½ cup (125 mL)	vegetable oil
½ cup (125 mL)	unsweetened cocoa powder *(total amount)*
½ cup (125 mL)	milk
1 tsp (5 mL)	vanilla
½ cup (125 mL)	chopped walnuts or pecans
1¾ cups (425 mL)	hot water

Preheat the oven to 350° F (180° C).

In an ungreased 9-inch (22 cm) square baking pan, stir together the flour, ¾ cup (175 mL) of the sugar (note: this is only *half* of the total amount of sugar), and the baking powder. In a small bowl, stir together the vegetable oil, and ¼ cup (50 mL) of the cocoa (this is *half* of the total amount of cocoa). Mix the cocoa mixture into the flour mixture, along with the milk and the vanilla. Stir with a fork until combined.

In another bowl, stir together the remaining ¾ cup (175 mL) of the sugar, the remaining ¼ cup (50 mL) of the cocoa, and the chopped nuts. Sprinkle this mixture over the stuff in the pan—don't mix it in. Now, carefully pour the hot water over everything—don't mess with it, don't stir it.

Bake at 350° F (180° C) for 40 to 45 minutes, until the top is crusty, but the sauce is bubbly. This is unbelievable served with vanilla ice cream.

Makes 6 servings, but I wouldn't count on it.

Rainy-Day Rice Pudding

Though recommended for rainy days, this rice pudding is also
suitable for blinding snowstorms, sleet, and even minor hurricanes—
as long as the power doesn't go out.

⅓ cup (75 mL)	*short grain* rice (this really does make a difference)
3 cups (750 mL)	milk, heated to *almost* boiling
¼ cup (50 mL)	sugar
2 tbsp (30 mL)	butter
¼ cup (50 mL)	raisins (optional)
1 tsp (5 mL)	vanilla
½ tsp (2 mL)	cinnamon

Preheat the oven to 250° F (120° C).

In a bowl, stir together the rice, the hot milk, the sugar, and the
butter. Pour into a greased 8-cup (2 liter) casserole dish. Bake at 250° F
(120° C) for about 2½ hours, stirring every half hour or so. Add the
raisins, if you're using them, in the last half hour of baking. Remove
from the oven and stir in the vanilla.

Serve warm or cold—sprinkled with the cinnamon, and (maybe
even) with a little milk or cream poured over it. Eat this while sitting in
a squishy chair, watching the rain drip down the window.

Makes 4 servings.

Crème Caramel

You want to make a sophisticated dessert—elegant, yet understated. Something that will give the impression that you actually know what you're doing, cookingwise. Something that appears tricky to produce but isn't. Here you go. No one will ever suspect.

¾ cup (175 mL)	sugar
2 tbsp (30 mL)	water
3	eggs
2½ cups (625 mL)	milk, heated until hot but not boiling
½ tsp (2 mL)	vanilla

Preheat the oven to 350° F (180° C).

In your smallest, heaviest skillet, cook ½ cup (125 mL) of the sugar with the water over medium heat, stirring constantly. First the sugar will dissolve, then the whole business will go all clumpy and weird, then— amazingly—the sugar will melt and turn golden and syrupy. Don't try to hurry this process because sugar can burn easily. Once it turns golden, remove the pan from the heat, let it cool for just a minute, and then pour evenly into the bottoms of 6 half-cup (125 mL) glass or pottery custard cups with flat bottoms. Set these aside.

Beat the eggs with the remaining ¼ cup (50 mL) of the sugar, then add the hot milk, stirring until the sugar is dissolved. Add the vanilla.

Pour the milk mixture into the sugar-lined custard cups (the sugar should be solidified). Set these custard cups into a baking pan large enough to hold them all, and pour enough boiling water into the pan to have it come about halfway up the sides of the cups. The idea here is to create a water bath around the custard cups so that they bake slowly and evenly. (As fancy cooking techniques go, this is one of the easier ones to do.) Put the entire pan (water and custard cups and all) into the oven, and bake at 350° F (180° C) for 50 minutes to 1 hour, or until a knife poked into the middle of one of the cups comes out clean, with nothing stuck to it.

Cool your crème caramels to room temperature, then refrigerate for several hours, or overnight. When you are ready to serve, run a thin knife around the edge of each custard to loosen it from its cup, then unmold each one onto a plate. The melted sugar will have mostly dissolved into a delicious caramel sauce, which you should pour over the custard.

Unbelievable. Makes 6 servings.

Bananas Flambé

Now, this is fun. Really fun. That it also happens to be an easy, delicious dessert is almost beside the point.

4	large, ripe bananas, peeled, cut in half crosswise, then split in half lengthwise
2 tsp (10 mL)	lemon juice
3 tbsp (45 mL)	butter
½ cup (125 mL)	brown sugar
3 tbsp (45 mL)	brandy or liqueur—any kind

Sprinkle the bananas with the lemon juice to prevent them from turning brown.

Now, melt the butter in a large skillet, and stir in the brown sugar. Add the bananas and cook them over medium heat until almost tender, about 3 minutes, turning them over carefully once. Remove from heat.

Put on your oven mitts and *turn off the lights*.

OK. Here's the good part. Pour the brandy or liqueur over the bananas (still in the skillet), and then immediately light a match (a long fireplace match keeps your hand away from the flame), and set the bananas on fire. Well, actually, it's just the brandy that ignites, but it's pretty exciting anyway. Enjoy the show, allow the flame to go out by itself, and then spoon the bananas and sauce over a dish of vanilla ice cream.

Makes 4 thrilling servings.

Apple (or Other) Crisp

Everyone knows about apple crisp. But what about peach, or rhubarb, or blueberry, or pear, or plum? Live on the edge—try a combination.

6	medium apples, peeled, cored and thinly sliced (about 4 cups/1 L of any fruit)
½ cup (125 mL)	sugar
½ tsp (2 mL)	cinnamon
½ cup (125 mL)	brown sugar
½ cup (125 mL)	butter or margarine, softened
½ cup (125 mL)	rolled oats
½ tsp (2 mL)	cinnamon

Preheat the oven to 375° F (190° C).

Dump the apple slices into a greased 9-inch (22 cm) square baking pan and add the sugar and the first ½ teaspoon (2 mL) of cinnamon. Toss together until well mixed.

In a bowl, combine the brown sugar, the softened butter, the oats, and the *second* ½ teaspoon (2 mL) of cinnamon, mashing them together with a fork until well mixed and crumbly. Sprinkle this over the apples in the pan. Bake at 375° F (190° C) for 35 to 45 minutes, until the apples are very soft when you poke a fork into the pan. You must serve this warm with vanilla ice cream. It's the law.

Leftovers (one can only hope) are an amazing breakfast.

Serves 6 to 8. Or less.

Baking Powder, Baking Soda—What's the Difference Anyway?

If the recipe calls for baking powder, *no*, you can't use baking soda instead. Or vice versa. Here's why: when you mix baking soda (also known as sodium bicarbonate) with an acid ingredient (such as vinegar, lemon juice, or yogurt) a chemical reaction takes place, creating little carbon dioxide bubbles that make your pancakes (for instance) nice and fluffy. Baking powder, on the other hand, is already a mixture of baking soda and an acid, so that it bubbles with no help whatever. In addition, baking powder also reacts to heat, causing it to double-bubble—once when you mix it into the batter, and again when you cook it. Each substance works differently, and shouldn't be substituted for the other. So pay attention!

Cinnamon Swirl Coffee Cake

Bake this cake and your house will smell unbelievable. And the cake is pretty good to eat too.

½ cup (125 mL)	sugar
2 tbsp (30 mL)	vegetable oil
1 tsp (5 mL)	vanilla
1	egg
1¼ cup (300 mL)	flour
2 tsp (10 mL)	baking powder
¾ cup (175 mL)	milk
½ cup (125 mL)	sugar
1 tsp (5 mL)	cinnamon

Preheat the oven to 350° F (180° C).

In a medium bowl, beat together the first ½ cup (125 mL) sugar, oil, vanilla, and egg just until well mixed.

In another bowl, stir together the flour and baking powder. Add the flour mixture and the milk alternately, by spoonfuls, to the egg mixture. Stir well.

Mix together the remaining ½ cup (125 mL) of sugar with the cinnamon.

Pour the batter into a well-greased 8-inch (20 cm) square baking pan and sprinkle with the cinnamon sugar. Using a knife, gently swirl the cinnamon sugar through the batter, folding it over in places, but leave it unevenly mixed. You should have some spots where the sugar is on the surface, and marbled into the batter in others.

Bake at 350° F (180° C) for 25 to 30 minutes, until the edges are browned, and a toothpick stuck in the middle comes out clean.

Serve warm or cold.

 # Instant Apple Pie

A fast, foolproof alternative to the real thing.

5	apples, peeled, cored, and thinly sliced
¼ cup (50 mL)	sugar
1 tsp (5 mL)	cinnamon
2 tbsp (30 mL)	butter
½ cup (125 mL)	sugar
1	egg
½ cup (125 mL)	flour
1 tsp (5 mL)	baking powder

Preheat the oven to 350° F (180° C).

Butter a 9-inch (22 cm) pie pan, and dump the apples into it. Sprinkle with the ¼ cup (50 mL) sugar and the cinnamon.

In a bowl, cream together the butter and sugar. Mix in the egg. Add the flour and baking powder, and stir until fairly smooth. Drop this batter, by spoonfuls, over the apples.

Bake at 350° F (180° C) for 45 minutes, or until the apples are soft and the topping is cooked.

There. Close enough, don't you think?

How to separate an egg and, more important, why

There are some recipes that ask you to do this. Why? Because in some dishes you may need only the yolk or only the white. You won't be doing this sort of thing often, but it's good to know how when you need to.

Find a medium-size funnel. (There's probably one in that scary junk drawer you hate.) Stand the funnel upright in a measuring cup, and *very carefully* crack the egg into it. Don't break the yolk! Lift the funnel up and gently shake it until the white slides out the hole, leaving the yolk stranded in the top. Dump the yolk out into one bowl, and the white into another. Repeat, if you need more than one egg separated.

Desperate for Cheesecake

*If this cheesecake is too much work for you, then you really aren't
quite desperate enough. Yet.*

Crust

1½ cups (375 mL)	graham cracker crumbs
¼ cup (50 mL)	sugar
⅓ cup (75 mL)	butter or margarine, melted

Filling

2 pkgs (250 g each)	cream cheese
½ cup (125 mL)	sugar
1 tsp (5 mL)	vanilla
2	eggs

Preheat the oven to 350° F (180° C).

In a bowl, stir together the graham cracker crumbs, sugar, and melted
butter. Press into the bottom and up the sides of a 9-inch (22 cm) pie
plate. If you happen to own 2 pie plates, squish 1 into the other with
the crumbs in between to get the crust really smooth and even.

In a large bowl, with an electric mixer, beat together the cream cheese,
sugar, and vanilla until well blended. Add the eggs, and keep beating
for another couple of minutes, until smooth. Pour into the crust. Bake
at 350° F (180° C) for 40 minutes—the center of the cheesecake will
still be a bit soft. Refrigerate at least 3 hours or overnight.

Top with fresh sliced strawberries, blueberries, peaches, or any kind
of ready-made pie filling. Purists, of course, may prefer to have it plain.

Makes 1 serving. Just kidding.

 # Pineapple Upside-Down Cake

Who thought this up anyway? Do you suppose it was an accident?

1 14-oz (398 mL)	can sliced pineapple rings (unsweetened)
2 tbsp (30 mL)	butter
½ cup (125 mL)	brown sugar
¼ cup (50 mL)	butter, softened
½ cup (125 mL)	sugar (regular white)
1	egg
1 tsp (5 mL)	vanilla
1 cup (250 mL)	flour
1½ tsp (7 mL)	baking powder

Preheat the oven to 350° F (180° C).

Drain the pineapple, saving the juice from the can in a small bowl.

Melt the 2 tbsp (30 mL) of butter and pour it into an 8-inch (20 cm) *square* baking pan or a 9-inch (22 cm) *round* baking pan. Add the brown sugar and 1 tbsp (15 mL) of the pineapple juice to the pan, stirring it around with a spoon until it's well mixed and coats the bottom of the baking pan. Arrange the pineapple slices as artistically as possible in the pan, cutting them in half if necessary (to achieve a suitably creative result).

In a bowl, with an electric mixer, cream together the butter and sugar until well mixed. Add the egg and vanilla, and beat until fluffy. In another bowl, mix together the flour and baking powder. Add the flour mixture by large spoonfuls alternately with ½ cup (125 mL) of the pineapple juice, beating after each addition. Spread the batter over the pineapple creation in the pan and bake at 350° F (180° C) for 40 to 45 minutes, until lightly browned.

While you're waiting, you can drink what's left of the pineapple juice.

When it's finished baking, remove cake from the oven. Let the upside-down cake (which is still right side up at this point) cool for 5 minutes, then run a knife around the edges of the pan to loosen it. Hold a plate over the pan and, all at once, flip the thing over. The upside-down cake should now be properly upside down, and your artwork should be clearly visible—if somewhat transformed. If any stubborn pineapple pieces remain clinging to the pan, just scrape them off and rearrange them on the cake. No one will know. Serve warm.

Makes 6 to 8 servings.

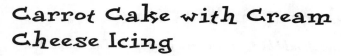

Carrot Cake with Cream Cheese Icing

Who else but a mom could possibly have thought to put carrots in a cake and cream cheese in the frosting?

2 cups (500 mL)	**flour**
2 tsp (10 mL)	**baking powder**
1½ tsp (7 mL)	**baking soda**
1 tsp (5 mL)	**cinnamon**
2 cups (500 mL)	**sugar**
1 cup (250 mL)	**vegetable oil**
4	**eggs**
2 cups (500 mL)	**grated carrots**
1 cup (250 mL)	**canned crushed pineapple, well drained**
½ cup (125 mL)	**chopped walnuts**

Preheat the oven to 350° F (180° C).

In a medium bowl, stir together the flour, baking powder, baking soda, and cinnamon. In a large bowl, combine the sugar, oil, and eggs, beating until smooth. Add the flour mixture to the egg mixture, stir, then add the carrots, pineapple, and walnuts. Pour this batter into a well-greased (or waxed-paper lined—see page 173) 9 × 13-inch (22 × 33 cm) baking pan, and bake at 350° F (180° C) for 40 to 45 minutes, or until a toothpick poked into the middle comes out clean.

Remove cake from the pan, and let it cool *thoroughly* on a rack before frosting with cream cheese icing. *Thoroughly.*

Cream Cheese Icing

¼ cup (50 mL)	**softened butter or margarine**
½ cup (125 mL)	**softened cream cheese**
2 cups (500 mL)	**icing sugar**

In a medium bowl, beat together all the ingredients until fluffy and smooth.

Makes enough icing to frost a 9 × 13-inch (22 × 33 cm) cake.

Chocolate Truffle Torte

This killer cake should be reserved for a very special occasion. You know: a birthday, an anniversary—that sort of thing. Don't make it too often, and never tell anyone how easy it was.

Cake:

4	eggs
¾ cup (175 mL)	sugar
⅓ cup (75 mL)	flour
2 tsp (10 mL)	cornstarch
¼ cup (50 mL)	unsweetened cocoa powder

Filling:

½ cup (125 mL)	raspberry jam
5 squares	semi-sweet baking chocolate (1 oz/28 g each) melted and cooled
1½ cups (375 mL)	whipping cream

Useless but fun

Remember the famous Volcano Project from Grade 4? You add some vinegar to some baking soda, and bingo! Instant Vesuvius! Try it—it'll make you feel like a kid again.

Preheat the oven to 350° F (180° C).

First, make the cake part. With an electric mixer, beat the eggs with the sugar on high speed until thick and light in color, about 5 minutes. Gradually add the flour, cornstarch, and cocoa powder. Pour into a greased and floured 9-inch (22 cm) springform pan, and bake at 350° F (180° C) for 25 to 30 minutes. Let cool, run a knife around the sides of the pan to loosen, and remove cake from the pan. Slice a thin layer from the top of the cake to flatten the surface. Chop the slice up into crumbs and set it aside. (Try not to eat it.) Put the rest of the cake back into the pan.

Spread the raspberry jam over the naked top of the cake layer in the pan. Pour the cold whipping cream into a large-ish bowl, and beat with an electric mixer until thick. Don't keep beating it after it's already whipped because you will end up with butter, which is very nice, but *not* what you want. Very carefully, fold the melted and cooled chocolate into the whipped cream, mixing gently but thoroughly. A few streaky parts are OK. Spread this over the raspberry layer. Sprinkle the crumbled cake bits over top of the chocolate whipped cream. Cover with plastic wrap and chill for at least 3 hours.

Just before serving, remove the sides of the springform pan and place the cake on a plate. You can sprinkle the top with icing sugar if you feel like it. But you don't have to.

Makes 8 to 10 spectacular servings.

How to Prepare a Cake Pan

Nothing is more annoying than a cake that refuses to exit the baking pan. Well, OK, there are some things that are more annoying—but not many. The following (unbelievably easy) method is guaranteed to help you avoid the dreaded Stuck Cake Syndrome.

Cut a sheet of waxed paper to fit your baking pan exactly. Use a pencil to trace around the pan and cut it precisely to fit. Now, lightly grease the pan (sides and bottom) with some solid vegetable shortening, butter, margarine, or cooking spray. Fit the waxed paper liner into the pan, and grease both the paper and the sides thoroughly.

That's all you have to do. Pour in the batter and bake the cake as usual.

To remove your cake from the pan, just run a knife around the sides of the cake, turn the pan over onto a metal rack or a platter, and the cake will drop right out. It really will drop right out. Peel off the paper, and away you go.

And no, the wax is not toxic.

How to measure butter or margarine

Measuring butter is one of those stupid jobs that no one likes to do. It sticks to the cup, it doesn't pack down easily, it's annoying. Here's a trick. Let's say your recipe asks for half a cup of butter. Fill a measuring cup to the half-cup level with cold *(important detail!)* water. Scoop in the butter, any which way, until it fills the cup all the way to the 1-cup mark. Drain off the water (completely) and voilà! You have a half cup of butter. Other amounts of butter will require you to do a little math. Naturally, this only works because the butter doesn't dissolve in water—don't try it with sugar, kids.

Almond Torte with Mocha Whipped Cream Icing

This recipe is not a mistake. It really works. Really.

4	**eggs**
¾ cup (175 mL)	**sugar**
1 cup (250 mL)	**whole almonds**
2 tbsp (30 mL)	**flour**
2½ tsp (12 mL)	**baking powder**

Preheat the oven to 350° F (180° C).

First, prepare two 8-inch (20 cm) round cake pans, by greasing them and lining them with waxed paper. See page 173 for details.

In a blender (you *really* do have to use a blender for this recipe), combine the eggs and sugar, and whirl at high speed until smooth. Now, add the almonds—yes, whole—put the lid back on the container, and blend until the nuts are very finely ground. Pulverized, actually. Now add the flour and the baking powder, and blend until combined. That's it.

Pour the batter into the prepared cake pans, and bake at 350° F (180° C) for about 15 minutes, or until lightly browned.

Let the cakes cool for about 5 minutes before you try to remove them from the pans. Then, run a knife around the side of the cake to loosen it from the pan, turn it over onto a metal rack (or, if you don't have one, a plate), and let it drop. It really will drop. Peel off the waxed paper and let the cake cool completely before icing it in an extremely elegant and tasteful manner.

Mocha Whipped Cream Icing

1½ cups (375 mL)	**whipping cream**
½ cup (125 mL)	**sugar**
¼ cup (50 mL)	**unsweetened cocoa powder**
2 tsp (10 mL)	**vanilla**
1 tbsp (15 mL)	**instant coffee**

Combine all the ingredients in a bowl and beat with an electric mixer until it's thick and forms peaks when you take out the beater.

This makes enough to spread generously on the top, sides, and between the two layers of an 8-inch (20 cm) round cake.

Don't forget to lick the beaters.

Idiotproof One-Bowl Chocolate Cake

It is probably possible for someone to mess this cake up. But you'd really have to work at it. Dark, rich, perfect.

1¾ cups (425 mL)	flour
2 cups (500 mL)	sugar
¾ cup (175 mL)	unsweetened cocoa powder
1½ tsp (7 mL)	baking powder
1½ tsp (7 mL)	baking soda
2	eggs
1 cup (250 mL)	milk
½ cup (125 mL)	vegetable oil
2 tsp (10 mL)	vanilla
1 cup (250 mL)	boiling water

Preheat the oven to 350° F (180° C).

Prepare two 8 or 9-inch (20 or 22 cm) round cake pans by lining them with waxed paper (see page 173 for foolproof details).

In a large bowl, combine the flour, sugar, cocoa, baking powder, and baking soda. Add the eggs, milk, oil, and vanilla, and beat with an electric mixer for about 2 minutes. You can, if you have to, do this by hand with a whisk. Pour in the boiling water, and mix just until combined.

Pour the batter evenly into the prepared pans, and bake at 350° F (180° C) for 30 to 35 minutes, until a toothpick stuck into the middle of each cake comes out clean.

Run a knife around the edge of each cake to loosen it from the pan, turn the pan over onto a metal rack (or a plate, if you don't have a rack) and the cake should just drop out. Peel off the waxed paper, and let the cake cool completely before icing. *Completely.*

Idiotproof One-Bowl Yellow Cake

The vanilla counterpart to the chocolate cake, this one is just as idiotproof, and just as good.

3	eggs
1½ cups (375 mL)	sugar
1½ tsp (7 mL)	vanilla
1½ cups (375 mL)	flour
1½ tsp (7 mL)	baking powder
¾ cup (175 mL)	milk, heated to boiling
3 tbsp (50 mL)	vegetable oil

Preheat the oven to 350° F (180° C).

Prepare two 8 or 9-inch (20 or 22 cm) round cake pans by lining them with waxed paper (see page 173 for foolproof details).

In a large bowl, with an electric mixer, beat the eggs for a few minutes, until foamy. Add the sugar and vanilla, and continue beating until light and fluffy, about 5 minutes.

Measure in the flour and baking powder, and beat just until combined. Finally, add the hot milk and vegetable oil, and beat until smooth.

Pour the batter evenly into the prepared pans, and bake at 350° F (180° C) for about 20 minutes, or until golden.

Loosen the sides of the cakes by running a knife around the edge, then turn them over onto a rack—they should fall out of the pans. Peel off the waxed paper, and let cool completely before icing.

Done.

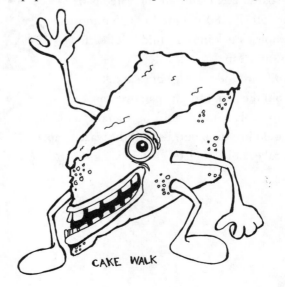

CAKE WALK

Frostings (Not from a Can)

*So there you are. You've made a cake from scratch. You're feeling
very proud of yourself. Now, are you really going to used a canned
frosting? I don't think so.*

Chocolate Buttercream Frosting

1 cup (250 mL)	**butter or margarine, softened**
½ cup (125 mL)	**unsweetened cocoa powder**
¼ tsp (1 mL)	**vanilla**
2 cups (500 mL)	**icing sugar (also known as confectioner's sugar)**
1 tbsp (15 mL)	**milk**

In a food processor, or in a large bowl with an electric mixer, beat the
butter until creamy. Add all the rest of the ingredients, and whip
together until very smooth.

If the icing seems too thick, add a little more milk, just a tablespoon
at a time, until it has the right consistency. Remember—you can always
add more milk, but you can't take it out if you've added too much.

Now really, that wasn't very difficult, was it?

This makes exactly the right amount of frosting to do a 2-layer, 9-inch
(22 cm) round cake, with just enough left over to lick off the beaters.

Vanilla Buttercream Frosting

1 cup (250 mL)	**butter or margarine, softened**
1 tsp (5 mL)	**vanilla**
3 cups (750 mL)	**icing sugar (also known as confectioner's sugar)**
2 tbsp (30 mL)	**milk**

In a food processor, or in a large bowl with an electric mixer, beat the
butter until creamy. Add all the rest of the ingredients, and whip
together until very smooth.

If the icing seems too thick, add a little more milk, 1 tbsp at a time,
until it has the right consistency.

There.

This makes exactly the right amount of frosting to do a 2-layer, 9-inch
(22 cm) round cake. Share the beaters with someone you like.

How to Make Whipped Cream

Whipped cream in a spray can may be piles of fun, but there is a better way. Not only does personally whipped cream taste much nicer, but it doesn't deflate and go all watery on your cake the way the spray stuff does.

Start with a container of *whipping cream* or *heavy cream*. Pour it into a bowl, add a spoonful or two of sugar, and using an electric mixer or a rotary hand mixer, whip the cream until it stands up in a soft peak when you lift the beater out. Stop beating as soon as it's whipped. If you continue, it will eventually turn into butter (did you know that?), which is not what you wanted, is it?

Helpful whipping hints: the colder everything is when you whip cream, the better it works. The cream should be straight from the refrigerator. And if you really want to go all out, put the bowl and the beaters in the fridge or freezer for a few minutes before whipping, too.

Snacks and Munchies

🍎🍐🌽🎃🧄🥬🥒🌭🌯🔭 🍩🧁🍞🍄🦪 🍳🥝🧆🥦🥖🍠🍶🧂

You roam the house like a starved cougar stalking its prey. You open a cupboard. The fridge. A drawer. Nothing good. Nothing. Well, you're just going to have to whip something up, aren't you?

High-Voltage Garlic Bread

Don't have this before a big date. Unless, of course, you've both been eating it.

1	long loaf Italian (or French) bread
4 to 6	cloves garlic, squished
2 tbsp (30 mL)	olive oil
2 tbsp (30 mL)	chopped fresh parsley
½ tsp (2 mL)	paprika
2 tbsp (30 mL)	grated Parmesan cheese

Preheat oven to 400° F (200° C).

In a small bowl, combine the garlic and oil, mashing them together well. In another bowl, mix together the chopped parsley, paprika, and Parmesan cheese.

Cut the bread in half crosswise, then as evenly as you possibly can, cut each half horizontally in half. This will give you 4 longish slabs of bread. Brush the garlic/oil mixture onto the cut surfaces of the bread, using it all up. Sprinkle, likewise, with the parsley mixture.

Put the breads on a baking sheet, and bake for 10 minutes, until lightly browned on top and heated all the way through. Oh please, oh please, oh please, don't leave the room while this is in the oven. In fact, don't answer the phone, don't read a book, don't do anything. Two minutes extra in the oven, and it's, um, toast. Or worse.

Cut diagonally into pieces and serve.

Makes 4 to 6 servings.

Dastardly Garlic Breadsticks

Dreadfully good, perilously addictive, and frighteningly easy to make.

1	**batch Absolutely Basic Yeast Dough (see recipe page 152)**
4	**cloves garlic, squished**
¼ cup (50 mL)	**vegetable oil**
1 tbsp (15 mL)	**coarse salt (also called pickling salt)**

Divide the dough into 4 blobs, and roll each into a long snake, no more than ½ inch (1 cm) thick. Cut the snake into 4 pieces, and arrange them on a greased baking sheet, making sure they don't touch each other.

Now, in a small bowl, mash the garlic into the vegetable oil. Brush the bread sticks with this mixture, then turn them over and brush them on the other side. Sprinkle evenly with the coarse salt.

Let the breadsticks rise (as in the bread recipe) in a warm place for 20 to 30 minutes. They won't have to rise too much, but they should get a little puffy.

Preheat your oven to 375° F (190° C), remembering to *take the breadsticks out of the oven first* if that's where you've put them to rise. Bake the breadsticks for 10 to 15 minutes, until the bottoms are lightly browned, and the top crust is golden.

These are best served straight from the oven, with soup or salad or dip. But they're good cold too, if there should be any left over (*as if*).

Makes about 16 dastardly breadsticks. Don't eat them alone.

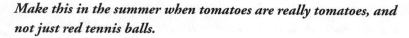

Bruschetta

Make this in the summer when tomatoes are really tomatoes, and not just red tennis balls.

1	long loaf French or Italian bread
¼ cup (50 mL)	olive oil
3	very ripe medium-size tomatoes
2	cloves garlic, squished
1 tbsp (15 mL)	vinegar or lemon juice
1 tbsp (15 mL)	chopped fresh parsley
1 tbsp (15 mL)	chopped fresh basil
1 tsp (5 mL)	salt

Chop the tomatoes as finely as you can, and combine them with the garlic, vinegar or lemon juice, parsley, basil, and salt. Go ahead and up the seasonings if you want.

Cut the bread crosswise into 2 halves, then cut each half horizontally into halves lengthwise. This will give you 4 long slabs of bread. Lay them, cut side up, on a large baking sheet. Using a pastry brush (or clean paintbrush) lightly brush the cut side of each slab of bread with the olive oil. Turn your oven to *broil*, set the baking sheet on the top rack, and toast the top of the bread for about 5 minutes, *just until golden brown*. Don't leave the room. One minute too long under the broiler, and it's charcoal.

When the bread is toasted, top with the chopped tomato mixture, cut into 3-inch (7 cm) sections, and serve.

This really makes about 4 or 5 servings as an appetizer, but you might just find yourself eating the whole works by yourself for dinner.

Pizza from the Ground Up

Make your own pizza and your friends will think you're brilliant. Make your own pizza with a homemade crust and they'll think you're a god.

The crust:

Begin with a batch of Absolutely Basic Yeast Dough (recipe on page 152). One batch is enough for 2 12-inch (30-cm) pizzas, *or* 1 single huge pizza. You can use half of the dough right away, and freeze the other half (tightly wrapped in plastic) to use later, or you can make 2 pizzas, bake one today, and freeze the other (unbaked) for a future pizza emergency.

Don't have time for this stuff? Desperate for pizza? Right now? Here are some other pizza crust possibilities:

- Italian flatbread shell
- French or Italian bread, cut in half lengthwise and lightly toasted under the broiler
- Frozen bread dough
- Fresh bread dough from a bakery
- English muffins
- Tortillas
- Pita bread

Creating the pizza:

The following ingredients are just suggestions, so don't take them too seriously. Add or subtract anything and everything—the actual procedure is the same no matter what you put on your pizza. The amounts, too, are extremely approximate.

1 cup (250 mL)	spaghetti sauce
2 cups (500 mL)	shredded mozzarella cheese
1 cup (250 mL)	sliced mushrooms
1 cup (250 mL)	sliced pepperoni
1 cup (250 mL)	crumbled, cooked bacon
½ cup (125 mL)	chopped green pepper
½ cup (125 mL)	chopped onion
½ cup (125 mL)	sliced olives
½ cup (125 mL)	pineapple chunks
1 tsp (5 mL)	oregano
½ tsp (2 mL)	hot pepper flakes

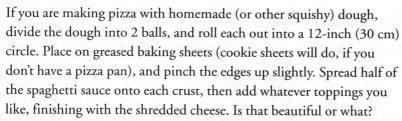

If you are making pizza with homemade (or other squishy) dough, divide the dough into 2 balls, and roll each out into a 12-inch (30 cm) circle. Place on greased baking sheets (cookie sheets will do, if you don't have a pizza pan), and pinch the edges up slightly. Spread half of the spaghetti sauce onto each crust, then add whatever toppings you like, finishing with the shredded cheese. Is that beautiful or what?

Slide your pizzas onto the lowest rack of the oven (did you remember to take out that bowl of water?) and bake at 425° F (220° C) for 20 minutes, or until the crust is browned and crisp underneath (peek under to check) and the cheese is melted and gooey. Midway through the baking time, you may have to transfer the pans to a higher oven rack to prevent the crust from burning before the topping is done.

Alternative pizza crusts (bready things that are already fully or partly baked) should be spread with sauce, sprinkled with toppings, and then baked. A pizza with a pre-baked crust will only need to be in the oven for as much time as it takes for the cheese to melt.

Makes two 12-inch (30 cm) pizzas or however many bigger or smaller ones.

Quesadillas

A serious snack, this actually comes dangerously close to being a meal.

Flour tortillas
Salsa
Cheese, any kind
Other toppings? Jalapeños? Olives? Chocolate
chips (just kidding).

Spread a flour tortilla with a generous layer of salsa—any kind, hot or mild. Top this with some shredded cheese and whatever other toppings, if any, you might want to add. Then slam another tortilla on top.

Place the tortilla "sandwich" in a dry skillet—no butter or oil or anything—and cook over medium heat, spinning once in a while to keep it from sticking, until the cheese begins to melt (lift an edge and peek inside). Using a pancake turner, flip the quesadilla over and cook the other side for 1 or 2 minutes, until the bottom begins to brown and the cheese inside is completely melted.

Slide the quesadilla out onto a plate, and cut into wedges like a pizza.

Logical variation: *Try this using spaghetti sauce instead of salsa, mozzarella cheese, and chopped pepperoni. Voilà! A Pizzadilla.*

Fully Loaded Nachos

Vegetarians may use refried or baked beans (canned or homemade) instead of the meat in these nachos. Or just leave it out to make a batch of Partially Loaded Nachos.

¾ lb (375 g)	ground beef
⅓ cup (75 mL)	salsa (mild or hot—however you like it)
4 cups (1 L)	tortilla chips
2 cups (500 mL)	shredded cheddar or Monterey Jack cheese

Crumble the ground beef into a skillet, and cook, stirring, over medium heat for 5 to 7 minutes, until no longer pink. *Or*, if you have a microwave, crumble the beef into a microwave-safe bowl, and zap it on high power for 4 to 6 minutes, stirring once or twice, until the meat is no longer pink. Either way, drain off the fat, and then stir in the salsa.

In a regular oven, arrange all the tortilla chips on a baking sheet and top, as evenly as possible, with the meat mixture. Sprinkle with the cheese. Bake at 400° F (200° C) for 10 minutes, just until the cheese is melted.

In a microwave oven, arrange the chips on 2 microwaveable plates, top with the meat mixture and the cheese, evenly divided between the two. Zap plates on high power, one at a time, for 1½ to 2½ minutes, until cheese is melted.

Add tomatoes, olives, sour cream, peppers, whatever. Or not. It's good any old way.

This makes enough Fully Loaded Nachos to ruin two people's appetites entirely for dinner.

A Swiss Fondue Evening

The snow swirls outside the window of your chalet (your basement apartment), high in the Swiss Alps (down the street from the city dump). A roaring fire blazes in the hearth (the electric heater is on). You gaze romantically (you hope you look romantic) into the eyes of You-Know-Who as you dunk your bread into the bubbling cheese (and pray that you don't drop it down your sleeve).

1	clove garlic, cut in half
2 cups (500 mL)	dry white wine
1 lb (500 g)	Swiss Emmentaler cheese, grated
3 tbsp (45 mL)	flour
dash	nutmeg and paprika
1	loaf crusty French or Italian bread, cut into 1-inch (2.5 cm) cubes

A fondue contraption usually consists of a medium-size pot, set over a small alcohol burner that can go on the table. It comes with a set of long-handled forks. These can be found by the gazillion at garage sales—very good places to get them. However, if you don't happen to have an Official Fondue Set, just use a heavy saucepan over low heat on the stove, and regular forks. It won't be quite as romantic, but it'll do the trick.

Rub the inside of your fondue pot (or saucepan) with the halved clove of garlic, then discard the garlic. If you are a real garlic fiend, you can chop up the clove and toss it into the pot (but they would never do that in Zurich). Pour the wine into the pot and heat it on the stove, over medium heat, but don't let it boil.

In a large bowl, mix the cheese with the flour and add it, by handfuls, to the wine, stirring constantly until cheese is melted. Bring this to a bubble for just a few seconds, then transfer the pot to the fondue burner (if you're using that), or simply lower the heat on the stove as much as possible so that the cheese is just barely kept at a simmer. Stir in the nutmeg and paprika.

To serve, spear a cube of bread on the fondue fork (or regular fork), swirl it in the cheese and eat. If you *(accidentally)* drop your bread into the pot, it is customary to kiss the person to your right. It is, however, considered bad form to deliberately unprong another person's bread.

Serves 2 to 4 dippers.

Focaccia Bread

Focaccia is like a pizza without the tomato sauce. If you've never made bread before, this is an easy place to start.

1 batch	**Absolutely Basic Yeast Dough** **(recipe on page 152)**
¼ cup (50 mL)	**olive or vegetable oil**
2	**onions, sliced**
4	**cloves garlic, squished**
¼ cup (50 mL)	**grated Parmesan cheese**
1 tsp (5 mL)	**crumbled, dried rosemary or oregano**
½ tsp (2 mL)	**salt**
¼ tsp (1 mL)	**pepper**

Divide the dough into 2 balls. Working with a blob of dough at a time, flatten it out into an 8-inch (20 cm) circle, about ½ inch (1 cm) thick. Place on a greased baking sheet, and repeat with the second blob.

Heat the oil in a skillet, add the onions and garlic, and cook over medium heat, stirring occasionally, for 5 to 7 minutes, until softened. Let the onions cool for a couple of minutes, then spread half of the mixture on each round of dough, leaving some bare dough around the edge. Sprinkle on the Parmesan cheese, rosemary or oregano, salt, and pepper, dividing everything more or less evenly between the two breads.

Let the breads rise (the way you did before) in a warm place for 20 to 30 minutes. It doesn't have to get *really* puffy—a *little* puffy is fine.

Preheat your oven to 375° F (190° C) remembering to **take the breads out of the oven first**, if that's where you've put them to rise. Bake the focaccia for 20 to 25 minutes, until the bottom is lightly browned, and the top crust is golden. This is best eaten while warm, but leftovers (*ha*) make an incredible sandwich.

Everyone will go nuts, so be prepared.

Makes 2 10-inch (30 cm) breads.

Mushrooms Masquerading as Escargots

Escargots (in case you don't already know this) are snails. Regular, ordinary, garden snails. Baked in garlic butter they taste delicious. But so would a pencil eraser. Imagine, then, what that same garlic butter could do for a mushroom.

½ cup (125 mL)	butter
2 tbsp (30 mL)	finely chopped onion
2 or 3	cloves garlic, squished
2 tbsp (30 mL)	finely chopped parsley
	salt and pepper
24	medium mushrooms, washed and with stalks removed

Preheat the oven to 375° F (190° C).

Melt the butter in a small saucepan, and add the chopped onion, garlic, and parsley. Stir, and remove from heat. Season with salt and pepper.

Arrange the mushrooms in a baking pan, gill side up, just big enough to hold them all. Pour the garlic butter over them, making sure the caps are filled. Bake at 375° F (190° C) for 15 to 20 minutes, until the mushrooms are softened. Serve hot with some crusty French bread.

Makes 3 or 4 servings.

Pita Crisps

Give your pita bread a second life! Reincarnate that stale package of pita as a crunchy snack. Easy, delicious, and everyone will think you're amazing.

Preheat the oven to 200° F (100° C).

Carefully split each pita bread into 2 separate layers, and spread them out on a large baking sheet, inside surface up. It really doesn't matter if you rip the breads—you'll be breaking them up afterward anyway.

Pour a little olive oil, vegetable oil, or melted butter into a small dish. Stir in a squished clove of garlic (2, if you're feeling wild). Using a pastry brush (or a clean paintbrush) lightly brush the rough surface of the pita breads with the garlic/oil mixture. Sprinkle with salt and pepper, and whatever other seasonings you like (oregano, cayenne, parsley, dill, etc.). Bake at 200° F (100° C) until crisp and golden—about 1 hour.

Break up the pita into smaller pieces, and serve with dips, salad, soup, or all by itself.

Do-It-Yourself Dips

Now, why would you go and buy a ready-made dip when it is so easy to make your own? The following dips are divinely delicious and diabolically easy to devour. Definitely.

Mustard Dip

¼ cup (50 mL)	mustard (is there any Dijon in the house?)
½ cup (125 mL)	sour cream (or half sour cream and
	half plain yogurt)
	salt, pepper, Tabasco sauce

Stir it all together.

Cheese Dip

2 cups (500 mL)	sour cream
1½ cups (375 mL)	shredded sharp cheddar cheese
¼ cup (50 mL)	pimento-stuffed olives
	salt and pepper to taste

Throw everything in the blender and whirl.

Dill Dip

1 cup (250 mL)	sour cream
½ cup (125 mL)	mayonnaise
1 tbsp (15 mL)	finely chopped fresh dill
1 tbsp (15 mL)	finely chopped green onion
1 tsp (5 mL)	lemon juice
	salt and pepper

Stir everything together, and refrigerate for an hour.

Curry Dip

½ cup (125 mL)	sour cream
½ cup (125 mL)	mayonnaise
2 tsp (10 mL)	curry powder
1	clove garlic, squished
	salt and pepper to taste

Stir it all together and dip.

Guacamole

Not only is this a great dip for tortilla chips, but it's also wonderful to glop onto a taco, and excellent to add to your nachos.

3	ripe avocados, halved, pitted, and peeled
1	medium tomato, finely chopped
1	clove garlic, squished
1	jalapeño pepper, finely chopped (sensitive souls may leave this out)
1	green onion, finely chopped
¼ cup (50 mL)	finely chopped cilantro or parsley (if you have it)
3 tbsp (45 mL)	lemon juice
¼ tsp (1 mL)	salt

Put the avocados into a bowl and mash them with a fork until they are mostly mashed, but still a little lumpy. Add all the other ingredients and stir them together until completely mixed. Taste, and adjust the seasoning if necessary.

Makes about 2 cups (500 mL) of guacamole.

Hummus

1 19-oz (540 mL)	can chick peas, drained (but save the liquid)
¼ cup (50 mL)	liquid from the can of chick peas
¼ cup (50 mL)	tahini (sesame paste—available at middle eastern and health food stores, and some supermarkets)
¼ cup (50 mL)	lemon juice
2	cloves garlic
½ tsp (2 mL)	ground cumin (optional)
	salt and pepper to taste

Put everything in the blender or food processor and zip it until really smooth, scraping down the sides 2 or 3 times. Taste, and adjust the seasoning, if necessary. Hummus should be a little thicker than, say, sour cream. If it's too thick, add another spoonful or two of chick pea liquid to loosen it up. Scoop into a bowl, sprinkle the top with a little chopped parsley and a drizzle of olive oil, and serve with pita bread or vegetable dippers.

Makes about 2 cups of hummus.

Chicken Liver Pâté

Liver gets no respect. But call it pâté, serve it with some fancy crackers, and oo la la!

2 tbsp (30 mL)	**butter**
1 or 2	**cloves garlic, squished**
1 lb (500 g)	**chicken livers, cut into halves**
1 tbsp (15 mL)	**finely chopped fresh parsley**
½ cup (125 mL)	**softened butter**
½ tsp (2 mL)	**salt**
¼ tsp (1 mL)	**pepper**

Heat the 2 tbsp (30 mL) of butter in a skillet, add the garlic, and cook over low heat until soft—about 2 minutes. Add the chicken livers, raise the heat to medium high, and cook, stirring them around in the pan, until browned on the outside but still a little pink inside when you cut them open—about 5 minutes. Add the parsley, cook for another minute, then remove from heat.

Scoop the livers (and all their juice) into the container of a blender or food processor, and add the ½ cup (125 mL) of softened butter, the salt, and pepper. Zip it around, scraping the sides down once in a while, until the mixture is completely puréed and smooth.

Pack the pâté into a small dish or crock, cover it with plastic wrap, and refrigerate at least 4 hours, or overnight. Serve with crackers or French bread. And your very best French accent.

Makes about 2 cups (500 mL) of pâté.

How to Make a Good Cup of Coffee

If you're planning to be an actual grownup, it's essential that you know how to make a good cup of coffee. This skill will allow you to appear sophisticated, profound, and slightly mysterious. It also helps to wear lots of black turtlenecks and write incomprehensible poetry. Mysterious poets don't drink instant.

The filter drip method is the easiest way to make good coffee. If you don't have an electric coffeemaker, you can get a simple plastic filter cone holder very cheaply at any housewares store, or even more cheaply at a garage sale. Buy filters to fit the cone, and a pot in which the finished coffee will collect. So much for equipment.

You'll also need to buy some coffee. There are a zillion different brands and flavors and types out there. Buy what you can afford. Fine or extra-fine grind, please, if you are using the drip method.

The method:

Place a clean paper filter into the filter holder of whatever type of coffeemaker you have. Into this, measure 1 tbsp (15 mL) ground coffee for each cup (250 mL) of coffee you will be making. If you have an electric drip coffeemaker, measure the corresponding amount of water into the water reservoir, and turn on the switch. Otherwise, measure the amount of water you need into a kettle or a saucepan, bring it to a boil, and then pour it *gently* over the ground coffee in the filter. Don't be in a hurry— allow the water to drip through gradually. Write a poem while you wait.

How to Make a Nice Cup of Tea

Everyone knows that tea drinkers are very tasteful, refined individuals. They listen to classical music, they go to the opera, and they practice tai chi. Maybe you are one. Or maybe you would just like a nice cup of tea, and skip the opera part. That's fine too.

Regular tea is made from the leaves of the tea bush, contains caffeine (just like coffee), and is what most people think of as tea. It is available in tea bags or loose, and in many different varieties, some with fruit flavors added to it. It may be called "orange pekoe" or "Earl Grey" or "Darjeeling" or some other such thing. Try several and see what you like.

Herbal teas are made from various herbs, fruits, and spices, and don't contain caffeine. They tend to have cool New Age names like "Mango Meditation" or "Nutmeg Nirvana." Because there are so many different kinds, you'll have to experiment to find which ones you like.

The method:

Fill your kettle, or a saucepan, with fresh, cold water. Bring it to a full boil. Meanwhile, rinse your cup or teapot out with hot water, and put in your tea bag or bags (assuming you are using tea bags, not loose tea). Use 1 tea bag for every 2 cups of boiling water. So, for example, if your teapot holds 4 cups of water, use 2 tea bags. Pour in the boiling water and let it steep for 5 minutes. Remove the tea bag(s) before serving.

Regular tea is usually served with milk and sugar. Some people prefer it with honey and lemon (no milk), or just plain with nothing. Herbal tea should be served with honey or sugar, but *never* with milk.

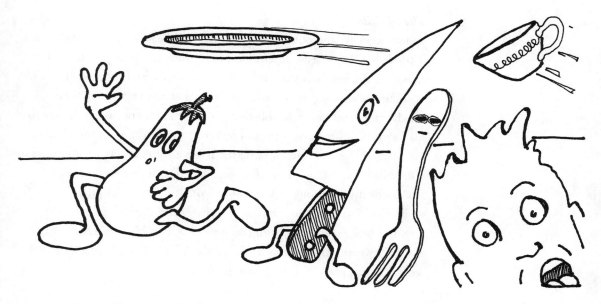

The Back of the Book

How to Plan a Meal

This is not about the kind of meal where you stand in front of the refrigerator, grab whatever happens to be at the front, and eat it while watching TV. No. This is about the other kind of meal. At a table. Maybe with friends. Served on plates. Eaten with a fork, even. Scary? It doesn't have to be.

The Beginning

This is the part that gets you interested and gives the cook time to (madly) finish making the rest of dinner. It might be some veggies and dip. It might be a bag of pretzels. Or it could be Beluga caviar on crackers (but not bloody likely). Don't go overboard on the starters unless you expect the main course to be inedible or terribly late, and try to avoid serving a food that will also appear elsewhere in the meal.

The Middle

Your basic meat and potatoes section, the middle is where you find your main dish. Of course, it doesn't have to be meat and potatoes. It can be lasagna and salad, beans and rice, or tuna casserole and broccoli. There's nothing really *wrong* with the usual formula of one meat thing, one starch thing, and one vegetable thing, except that it's not the only way to plan a meal. Try to vary tastes and textures, but don't attempt to make too many different dishes because you'll drive yourself crazy. Sometimes one really great dish with a loaf of good bread is all you need.

Artistically speaking, avoid monochromatic meals. A dinner of white chicken, white potatoes, and white cauliflower might taste just fine, but looks really depressing on a plate. An all-black dinner is usually even worse. And, unless it's St. Patrick's Day, a totally green meal would be just plain weird. Go multicolor.

The End

The part everyone has (secretly) been waiting for. Oh sure, they were polite through the meat loaf. But they were *really* thinking about dessert. Will it be a Chocolate Truffle Torte? Will it be spectacular Bananas Flambé? Or will it be (drat) sensible, nutritious fruit? Most of the time you should probably go the sensible and nutritious route. But once in a while something gooey and unhealthful is very therapeutic.

Menus for Entertaining

The artsy vegetarian boy/girlfriend

Antipasto—arranged very artistically, with at least a couple of really weird items

Pasta with pesto

Sliced tomatoes with basil and olive oil

Very good Italian bread

Fresh fruit—the more exotic the better

The intellectual boy/girlfriend

Pita crisps with hummus

Irish lamb stew

Cole slaw with un-creamy dressing

Cornbread

Crème caramel

Conservative but intriguing girl/boyfriend

Mushrooms pretending to be escargots

Curry glazed chicken

Plain cooked couscous

Steamed fresh asparagus

Cucumber salad

Pineapple upside-down cake

Shallow but fun boy/girlfriend

Veggies and dip

Spaghetti with meatballs

Bruschetta

Green salad with desperation ranch dressing

Brownies with ice cream

Desperately, madly (almost stupidly) in love

Smoked oysters (from a can) with crackers

Spinach soup

Swiss fondue

An extremely interesting green salad with vinaigrette dressing

Chocolate mousse torte

The thrill is gone dinner

Tortilla chips with salsa

Potato and hot dog paprikash

Cole slaw with creamy dressing

Peanut butter cookies

Mom and Dad for dinner (with optional younger siblings)

X-ray vision soup

Incredible garlic chicken

Steamed broccoli

Plain cooked rice

Romaine lettuce salad with vinaigrette dressing

French bread

Carrot cake

Your best friend is depressed

Minestrone soup

Focaccia

A big salad with slightly Caesar dressing

Self-saucing hot fudge pudding with ice cream

Your sweetie has a cold (awwwww)

Chicken soup with noodles

Irish soda bread (just out of the oven, of course)

Earl Grey tea

Rice pudding

Buncha galoots over for supper

Veggies with dips (plenty of everything)

Lasagna

Real garlic bread

Mixed green salad with creamy Italian dressing

Chocolate cake with chocolate icing

Happy birthday to yooooo!

Homemade pâté with crackers

Hawaiian meatballs

Plain rice

Mixed green salad with Zorba the Greek dressing

Almond mocha torte

Video watch-a-thon evening (also suitable for big sports things on TV)

Fully loaded nachos

Chicken wings

Veggie sticks with mustard dip

Homemade pizza

Idiotproof yellow cake with chocolate icing

Slightly sophisticated brunch

Gazpacho

Cheese and bread overnight wonder

Chunky pasta salad

Banana bread, cinnamon coffee cake

Aunt Gladys for lunch

Potato soup

Unfettered frittata

Absolutely normal lettuce salad with slightly Caesar dressing

Good Italian bread

Fresh fruit—regular things like oranges, grapes, peaches, apples

Cooking Terminology Demystified

Mince, sauté, deglaze—what exactly are they asking us to do, and is it decent?

Bake To cook in an oven. You know—like a cake.

Baste Like applying sunscreen at the beach, you baste foods like turkey to keep them moist while they're roasting.

Beat To clobber the daylights out of, let's say, an egg. Can be done by hand with a whisk or fork, or in an electric mixer.

Blend To combine ingredients into a uniform mixture.

Boil Scientifically speaking, to bring a liquid to 212° Farenheit (100° Celsius) until it gets hot and bubbly.

Braise To cook slowly, with a little liquid, in a covered pan.

Bread To coat a food in bread crumbs before frying—like chicken or fish.

Broil Under the broiler—sort of like an upside-down barbecue.

Chop To cut up into little pieces. Bigger than minced, but smaller than diced. OK?

Cream To mush together soft ingredients, like butter and sugar, to make a creamy mixture.

Curdle A disgusting effect that happens to certain sauces when they are overcooked—yucky, lumpy, separated clumps.

Dash Oh, just a squirt or two.

Deglaze You deglaze a pan by pouring a little liquid into it, then cooking to dissolve the brown bits stuck on the bottom. Makes a nice gravy, and saves on dishwashing.

Dice Bigger than chopped (see above). Usually in little sort-of-square shapes.

Dredge To lightly coat a food with flour or crumbs. You wouldn't have guessed that, would you?

Drizzle What happens when you forget your umbrella. Just kidding. Actually, to pour a thin stream of liquid over food.

Drop What a person asks for when they really want more. As in "I'll just have another tiny *drop* of lasagna."

Dunk What you do to your chocolate chip cookie in a glass of milk.

Fold To very gently mix one ingredient into another using a spatula to lift from underneath. Don't try to do this when you're in a big hurry.

Fry The f-word. To cook food in a pan with plenty of oil, resulting in either delicious crispness, or greasy sog. Depending.

Garnish That little sprig of parsley beside the mashed potatoes. The slice of orange next to the chicken. The paprika on the potato salad. Most commonly found in restaurants, where they have time to do this sort of thing.

Grate To put through the holes of a grater, usually resulting in shreddy little pieces. Cheese is the most common victim of this process. Also knuckles. Be careful.

Grease To coat a pan with, yes, *grease*, so that food doesn't stick.

Julienne Thin strands of any kind of food that doesn't naturally occur in that shape—such as long strings of carrot or zucchini or ham.

Knead To mangle a lump of dough by hand in order to make it smooth and uniform. Usually associated with bread dough. Excellent for venting frustration.

Leavening Any substance that is used to cause a mixture to rise while baking—like yeast or baking powder.

Marinate To soak food in a liquid in order to tenderize or add flavor.

Mash To squash with a fork or masher. Made famous by potatoes.

Melt To turn a solid into a liquid. Sometimes, unfortunately, it happens by accident to your ice cream cone.

Meringue The best part of a lemon pie. A fluffy substance made of stiffly beaten egg whites and sugar.

Mince Smaller than *either* diced or chopped (see above). Little eensy bits.

Mix Just stir it together, with a spoon or fork or your hands or a shovel. Depending.

Peel To remove the outside of a fruit or vegetable, the part that your mother always told you has all the vitamins.

Pinch YOW! Don't *do* that! Just a tiny bit more than a dash (see above).

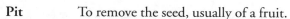

Pit   To remove the seed, usually of a fruit.

Poach   To cook in gently simmering (see below) water.

Pound   What you'd like to do to that idiot who wrecked your bike. In food, to flatten.

Preheat To turn your oven on ahead of time so that it will be at the right temperature when you put the cake in.

Purée   To mash or blend a solid food into a smooth, lump-free mixture.

Roast   Really, this is the same as bake (see above) except that it's generally associated with meat. You wouldn't, for example, *roast* a cake.

Sauté   But of course, zees ees to cook zee food in zee pan weeth just a leetle bit of zee oil or zee butter. Ooo la la.

Scorch   What happens when you go answer the phone while your spaghetti sauce is boiling, resulting in a black residue on the bottom of the pot, a nasty burned taste and smell, and a lot of bad words.

Scramble What you do to an egg with a fork.

Shred   To cut or grate something into long thin pieces.

Sift   What you do to flour in order to remove any lumps and to fluff it up.

Simmer   Almost boiling, *but not quite.*

Sliver   A thin strip. *Except* when used in the following sentence: "I'll have just a *sliver* of pumpkin pie," when it means a huge slab.

Squish   Unofficial terminology—what you do to a clove of garlic (see page 48).

Steam   To cook food in a basket or strainer suspended over (but not touching) boiling water. Especially useful for vegetables.

Stew   To cook something for a long time, in a covered pan with some liquid.

Stir   To mix with a spoon.

Stir-fry Tossing and stirring cut-up bits of food in a pan with hot oil. Very fast, very dramatic. Also very messy, if you're not careful.

Stock   Broth, basically. Can be made with meat or vegetables or fish.

Strain To remove the solid bits from a liquid. You know—like when you have those floaty little things you hate in your orange juice.

Toss Mixing enthusiastically! Yahoo!

Whip Like beat (see above) but even *more* so. You do this to cream and egg whites.

Whisk To beat with a (*surprise*) whisk. What you do to a sauce, for instance, to get the lumps out.

Zest The colored outside peel of an orange or lemon.

The Clueless Guide to Metric Conversion

OK, so Great-Aunt Bertha *finally* gives you the secret recipe for her Double Chocolate Overload Cake. You look at it and—drat—it's not in metric. Or you go out to buy a pound of hamburger and discover that the store has everything marked in grams. Or—eek—your measuring cup is metric and the recipe you want to use calls for ⅔ cup. Now what do you do? Well convert, of course. Wait—don't go away—it's not that hard.

Unless you happen to be a nuclear physicist, it's not necessary to convert cooking measurements *exactly*. Close is usually good enough. The table below will give you both imperial and U.S. measurements, with both the approximate metric equivalent and the exact conversion. If you happen to be engaged in vertex tracking of solar neutrino double beta gravitation, then you really ought to use exact measurements. However, for normal cooking, the approximate metric equivalent will be just fine.

But first, a couple of quick and dirty conversion methods:

- To convert ounces to milliliters, multiply the number of ounces by 30. This will give you something *close* to the right answer—good enough for cookies.
- To convert milliliters to ounces, drop the last digit and divide by 3.

Metric Conversion Table

Canadian (imperial) unit	U.S. unit	Approximate metric equivalent	Exact metric equivalent
1 imperial gallon 160 fluid ounces 4 imperial quarts	1 U.S. gallon 128 fluid ounces 4 U.S. quarts	4 litres	454 mL in imperial gallon 378 mL in U.S. gallon
1 imperial quart quart 40 fluid ounces 5 cups	1 U.S. quart 32 fluid ounces 4 cups	1 litre	1136 mL in imperial 946 mL in U.S. quart
1 imperial pint 20 fluid ounces 2½ cups	1 U.S. pint 16 fluid ounces 2 cups	1/2 litre 500 mL	568 mL in imperial pint 472 mL in U.S. pint
1 cup 8 fluid ounces 16 tablespoons	1 cup 8 ounces 16 tablespoons	250 mL	227 mL
½ cup 4 fluid ounces 8 tablespoons	½ cup 4 fluid ounces 8 tablespoons	125 mL	114 mL
⅓ cup	⅓ cup	75 mL	78 mL
¼ cup 2 fluid ounces 4 tablespoons	¼ cup 2 fluid ounces 4 tablespoons	50 mL	60 mL
1 tablespoon 3 teaspoons	1 tablespoon 3 teaspoons	15 mL	15 mL
1 teaspoon	1 teaspoon	5 mL	5 mL
½ teaspoon	½ teaspoon	2 mL	2.5 mL
¼ teaspoon	¼ teaspoon	1 mL	1.25 mL
1 pound 16 ounces	1 pound 16 ounces	500 grams	453 grams
2 pounds	2 pounds	1 kilogram	907 grams
½ pound 8 ounces	½ pound 8 ounces	250 grams	227 grams
¼ pound 4 ounces	¼ pound 4 ounces	125 grams	113 grams

Canadian (imperial) unit	U.S. unit	Approximate metric equivalent	Exact metric equivalent
200° fahrenheit	200° fahrenheit	100° celsius	93° celsius
250° fahrenheit	250° fahrenheit	120° celsius	121° celsius
275° fahrenheit	275° fahrenheit	140° celsius	135° celsius
300° fahrenheit	300° fahrenheit	150° celsius	148° celsius
325° fahrenheit	325° fahrenheit	160° celsius	162° celsius
350° fahrenheit	350° fahrenheit	180° celsius	176° celsius
375° fahrenheit	375° fahrenheit	190° celsius	190° celsius
400° fahrenheit	400° fahrenheit	200° celsius	204° celsius
425° fahrenheit	425° fahrenheit	220° celsius	218° celsius
450° fahrenheit	450° fahrenheit	230° celsius	232° celsius
200° fahrenheit	200° fahrenheit	100° celsius	100° celsius
8 inch pan	8 inch pan	20 centimetre pan	
9 inch pan	9 inch pan	22 centimetre pan	
10 inch pan	10 inch pan	25 centimetre pan	
9 × 13 inch pan	9 × 13 inch pan	22 × 33 centimetre pan	
10 × 15 inch cookie sheet	10 × 15 inch cookie sheet	30 × 40 centimetre cookie sheet	

Index